Foreword by Rachel G. Scott

Letters to a WEARY TRAVELER

A Journey of Lessons and God's Truth

SUE CONOVER

Book Published by Sue Conover, LLC.
P.O. Box 179 Aurora, OH 44202

© 2022 by Sue Conover
All rights reserved. Published 2022

The material in appendix 1 is from HelpGuide.org and is used by permission.

Printed in the United States of America
24 23 22 21 20 19 18 17 16 1 2 3 4 5 6

ISBN-13 (trade paper): 978-0-9980330-8-2
ISBN-13 (ebook): 978-0-9980330-1-3

Library of Congress Cataloging-in-Publication Data has been applied for.

Unless otherwise indicated, all Scripture quotations are taken from the Holy Bible, New Living Translation, copyright © 1996, 2004, 2007 by Tyndale House Foundation. Used by permission of Tyndale House Publishers, Inc., Carol Stream, IL 60188. All rights reserved.

Some scripture quotations are from the Holy Bible, New International Version, NIV, Copyright © 1973, 1978, 1984, 2011 by Biblica, Inc. Used by permission of Zondervan. All rights reserved worldwide. www.zondervan.com

Some scripture quotations are from the Giant Print Classic Reference Bible, King James Version, KJV, Copyright © 1994 by Zonervan Corporation. Used by permission of Zondervan. All rights reserved worldwide. www.zondervan.com

No part of this publication may be reproduced, stored in a retrieval system, or transmitted in any form or by any means—electronic, mechanical, photocopy, recording, or otherwise—without prior written permission of Sue Conover.

Editor: A'ndrea McAdams

Cover and Interior: RGSGroup.media

TABLE OF CONTENTS

Foreword 1

Introduction. 3

Chapter 1: Jesus' Blood Is "Red-Out". 9

Chapter 2: Christ, the Innocent One 19

Chapter 3: Worship 31

Chapter 4: Incense and Prayers. 43

Chapter 5: Healing the Lame Beggar 53

Chapter 6: "Peter, Do You Love Me?". 65

Chapter 7: My Lesson in Love 77

Chapter 8: Questioning God After Defeat 83

Chapter 9: God's Building Project 93

Chapter 10: Standing Up for God Against Giants 109

Chapter 11: Where God Chooses to Dwell 123

Chapter 12: Story of Daniel. 135

Chapter 13: Don't Worry About Your Life 149

Chapter 14: Bread and Water in the Wilderness. 163

FOREWORD

Walking in the assignment that God has given us can be challenging. But it is even more challenging when that assignment calls us to speak an uncompromising truth into a culture that advocates for the complete opposite. I have had to do this more than once, and what I have found is that we can never fully know what's on the other side of that act of courageous obedience. However, we do know that God is pleased with us when we choose obedience rather than conformity.

In this book, Sue walks us through stories, both personal and biblical, that will help us to courageously live out our faith during difficult times.

There are so many things that can cause us to grow weary along our journey. As I read *Letters to the Weary Traveler*, I reflected on my own life, story, and moments when I allowed weariness to lead. But there was always a moment along the way when God would remind me that I could exchange my weariness for His strength.

And this same invitation is extended to you.

Sue, in her loving, passionate and bold way, points us back to truth and holiness to help us become strengthened in our walk. The unique delivery of each *letter* allows us to identify areas within ourselves that need to be sharpened and shaped so that we can become a better reflection of Christ.

As you read *Letters to the Weary Traveler*, I pray that you are reminded of the strength you carry as a beloved child of God.

*-Rachel G. Scott, Founder of the
I Can't Come Down movement*

INTRODUCTION

When you spend time studying the Bible and read about the men and women of the Old and New Testaments, do you find you have more questions after you're done than when you started out?

This was my experience for many years. The times and cultures in the Bible were so different, and sometimes there is so much information that is left out about what was happening. I found it was so hard to relate and apply to my life and situation. I knew that these people and their experiences were supposed to instruct and teach me lessons, but I just couldn't understand how.

Now, however, I know the Lord wants to speak to each one of us in an individual and uniquely personal way every day. He wants to draw us into an intimate relationship with Him and share His heart with us through His words that are pertinent and needed for what we are going through right now. He wants us to understand how He thinks and sees things here in our lives on Earth and to impart His insight into our trials and struggles. His Word is alive and full of power. It is multidimensional and timeless. He uses it to work exactly what is needed for the person and time, whether 2,000 years ago, last year, or today. It really is the Living Word, literally!

Isn't that exciting and amazing?

We can read and speak the Word, and it is quickened and creates powerful changes and miracles in our situations and in our hearts. There are no boundaries or limits of space or time; it is outside these. God's plan was for His Word to be applied every day to everyone for everything. It's like a letter that the Lord, our loving Father, wrote just this morning just to you, and it relates to exactly what you are going through. He speaks to give you peace, assurance, insight, and direction—everything you need right now.

The Lord wants this to be how His Word works and transforms you every day of your life.

In the past, I studied Scripture, thought about what the verses meant, and tried to understand who the people were who the Lord was talking about. They were real people who lived many years ago, but I didn't really relate to them. They were all so different and unique in their cultures, beliefs, and stories.

There were a lot of men and women in the Bible who were considered doubters, scoffers, rebellious, and stiff-necked. Men with hard hearts and cruel thoughts and actions, and those who hated God. There were unbelievers and those who didn't trust God. Such men were self-righteous and thought they were good; they didn't think they needed to be saved from their sins and wickedness. I believed that these characters were the men and women who were surely going to hell. I was always quick to judge them.

Then the Bible talks about the righteous, faithful children of God who were men and women who followed the Lord and believed and trusted in Him: the prophets and saints of the Old and New Testaments. These were the believers like me, walking with the Lord and on their long journey to a heavenly home to be with Jesus, for eternity.

I never really related to the "bad characters" and the men of God who fell into sin in the Bible. I was very critical and judgmental toward all their failures and evil behavior.

Then the Lord started to show me that I had been just like all the characters in the Bible, good and bad, at different times in my life. I started to take a sober look at these characters, and I realized that the Lord was right. I was overwhelmed with the reality of God's mercy, grace, kindness, and patience toward all sinners, including me. I started to realize His limitless love and faithfulness toward me every day.

The Bible is not a window for me to look through to see other people but a mirror that reflects my own sinful image. I am guilty of all the same sins, and there have been times when I was evil and rebellious against God. Paul describes all the believers in this way: "And you, that were sometime alienated and enemies in *your* mind by wicked works, yet now hath he reconciled" (Colossians 1:21, KJV, emphasis mine).

I was an enemy of God before I was saved at 27 years old.

I was a scoffer, rebellious, and stiff-necked. When I came to Jesus, surrendered my life, and let Him be Lord of my heart, my behavior didn't change right away in some areas. I was fearful, and my faith was weak. I didn't trust the Lord. I was always anxious about the future and the circumstances that I was going through. I grumbled and complained a lot to the Lord, accusing Him of not caring and not loving me, just like the Israelites in the wilderness accused Him. Similarly, I was always speaking words of doubt and unbelief. I also was very critical and judgmental of other people and was quick to speak words of slander and gossip. I was a very carnal Christian.

All the things of the world—social activities, worldly success, and material things—were very attractive to me. I believed the lie that if I had them, I would be happier and enjoy life more. Most of my prayer life revolved around prayer for the things I wanted and thought I needed. Take your pick of anyone in the Bible, and I know that I have acted and thought just like them at some time in my life. To see these things about myself might have been very depressing. In reality, it has set me free, because I know that Jesus has forgiven me and washed all my sins away, that they are covered by His blood. He is able to transform me, and because He has paid the price in full for all my sins, past, present, and future, I am declared holy and blameless in His sight right now.

Jesus has promised to keep me strong to the end so that I will be blameless on the Day of our Lord Jesus Christ.

"His divine power has given us everything we need for life and godliness through our knowledge of him who called us by his own glory and goodness" (2 Peter 1:3, NIV).

God calls and equips. It's His power that will manifest through our lives. He will shine His light into every place.

Before I was shown these truths about myself, I believed the lie and delusion that I was "a good person," and with it came the constant pressure and burden to maintain that "goodness." If I slipped or fell, the Lord wouldn't think I was good anymore. The Lord never thought that I was good. All my self-righteousness is filthy rags. He never had those expectations of me. He gave His Son, Jesus, and through Him, I am made good and perfect. Jesus is the One who makes me righteous and accepted by the Father.

The Lord sees me in all my brokenness and loves me anyway.

He is committed to making me righteous and spotless. Through His grace, mercy, and power, I can rest in Him and live a life free from the worry to perform and measure up. My heart is full of thanksgiving and praise to Him, and my testimony is about the amazing things that the Lord has done for me, by His grace and power. He is working in me, to will and to do His good pleasure (see Philippians 2:13). He gets all the glory.

Now when I study and read the Bible, I ask the Holy Spirit to open the eyes of my heart and show me the deep and hidden things in His Word by teaching me the meaning of the scriptures. As I read, the verses open up to me, and the Lord shows me amazing insights and revelation into the people and events, and I can see myself in the story. This brings insight and understanding that I can apply to my life and the people around me in the struggles of today.

All the men and women in the Bible have struggled with the same issues and problems. They experienced the good and bad, victories, failures, trials, and sorrows.

My hope is that as you read this book, you will be inspired and empowered. I pray that the Lord will begin to speak personally to you and share His heart with you. May His Word literally come alive in your hands so that you will begin to experience more freedom and victory in your life. My prayer is also that your relationship with the Lord will become more than you could ever dream or imagine.

Chapter 1

JESUS' BLOOD IS "RED-OUT"

Have you ever used a product that covers errors and mistakes that are written on paper? I always write everything out first with pen and paper. So I have a bottle of liquid correction product handy because I am always making mistakes. I apply a little of it and miraculously the mistake is covered and never seen again.

Jesus' blood does so much more; it completely removes all that is recorded in God's book against us. It is the "red-out" for the books in heaven that contain the records of all our offenses and transgressions.

"And I saw the dead, small and great, stand before God; and the books were opened: and another book was opened, which is the book of life: and the dead were judged out of those things which were written in the books, according to their works" (Revelation 20:12, KJV).

"As I looked, thrones were set in place, and the Ancient of Days took his seat. His clothing was as white as snow; the hair of his head was white like wool. His throne was flaming with fire, and its wheels were all ablaze. A river of fire was flowing, coming out from before him. Thousands upon thousands attended him; ten thousand times ten thousand stood before him. The court was seated, and the books were opened" (Daniel 7:9-10, NIV).

I have this beautiful picture of the books in heaven being opened when we come to Him, asking for forgiveness. Then I see Jesus standing with the book in His hands and with a heart full of love, mercy, and compassion. He is touching the page with His blood-stained finger, sliding it right across the words and deeds we are guilty of, as if they never happened.

He blots them all out with one touch of His finger: "Blotting out the handwriting of ordinances that was against us, which was contrary to us, and took it out of the way, nailing it to his Cross" (Colossians 2:14, KJV).

Our hope—and what we as believers strive for—is to get to heaven, and when God opens His book with our name written on the cover, the pages will be all white and clean.

Did you know there was another book? It is our personal record book of sins done to us here on Earth. Most of us do not actually write them down in a book, but they are accurately stored and recorded in our hearts. So it is important to consider that it will be the measure that He will use to judge us for everything that we have recorded as unforgiven or unforgiveable in our book.

I know it is extremely hard to accept this truth about forgiving the unforgivable, but He never said that we had to do it in our own strength or ability. He wants us to be willing to turn them over to Him so He can work a miracle in our heart, so we can be free to forgive.

When He opens our record book, will He also find that the pages are white and clean because we have applied the blood of Jesus to the stains of others' sin done to us?

"For if you forgive other people when they sin against you, your heavenly Father will also forgive you. But if you do not forgive others their sins, your Father will not forgive your sins" (Matthew 6:14-15, NIV).

The Lord's Prayer says, "forgive us our debts, as we forgive our debtors" (Matthew 6:12, KJV).

"With the measure you use, it will be measured to you" (Luke 6:37, NIV).

So how can we forgive others who have cruelly and deliberately hurt us? Jesus said, "But I say unto you, Love your enemies, bless them that curse you, do good to them that hate you, and pray for them who despitefully use you, and persecute you" (Matthew 5:44, KJV).

We cry out, "How can I do this, Jesus?"

"With man this is impossible, but with God all things are possible" (Matthew 19:26, NIV).

We need to take a closer look at our hearts and be willing to have the Holy Spirit shine His light on the dark place where we hide our secret sins, bitterness, evil thoughts, and wrong attitudes from God.

We do not want to deal with them because of fear. We think that maybe someday in the future we will be stronger and able to open our hearts. The problem is that we will never be stronger because these very "wounds" are draining our strength and making us weaker each day.

This was my story for many years. I looked good on the outside, and I would daily spend time with the Lord. I prayed a lot and humbly asked for forgiveness for sins like unkindness, impatience, and critical words or actions I had done against people in my life. I wanted to keep the pages of the record book in heaven clean and stain free. I trusted Jesus and His shed blood to wash me white as snow.

However, all the while, I was keeping my own record book, and I held on to many of the offenses and debts that people owed me. I did not know that I would be judged exactly the same way as I had recorded the offenses against me, as I had judged them.

I knew that God was keeping a record in heaven of all the evil deeds done to me, and I wanted the offenders to be punished. So just in case God missed something, I was keeping my own records to use against them. I reminded Him in prayer regularly and even prayed for God to cause them harm and punish them now. I was well versed in the Old Testament and the psalms, and I knew what God had done to the enemies of the Israelites. I thought that I was well within my rights as a child of God to ask

Him to do this. I did not realize that my enemies were Satan and his demonic forces behind the person, not the person that Satan had used to inflict the evil against me.

I was like James and John, the disciples who asked Jesus, "Do you want us to call fire down from heaven to destroy them?" (Luke 9:54, NIV).

The evil and trauma that had been done to me were carefully stored away behind a closed door, along with all the poison and unforgiveness. The sign posted on the door read, "Keep out," and that meant everyone, even God!

Never would I have believed that what was hidden in that closet of my heart was the very thing that was making me sick and weak spiritually, emotionally, and physically. I was trying to keep my enemies locked out, but instead I was really locking the real enemy in. I did not know that the Lord was loving and powerful enough to deal with everything behind that door. I could not imagine how God could ask me to pray for my enemies so they would be forgiven and God would cancel all the punishment they deserve. What they did cost me parts of my life. The price tag on the debt they owed me was extremely high. If it were dollars, it would be millions.

The Father in His love and mercy and grace did not let me keep the door to this closet closed.

He spoke to my heart so that I would be willing to pray and open the door so His light could shine in. Like a laser beam, the Lord shined into every dark corner until the whole room was filled with the light of the Holy Spirit. I wanted to be set free from all the attitudes, beliefs, and patterns of thinking. I knew that my mind and thoughts were not the mind of Christ. Everything had to go; this closet needed to be thoroughly cleaned and emptied. All anger, malice, hate, and unforgiveness had to be removed so that God could fill it with His healing power and transform it into a holy place of worship and praise.

The Lord let me come to the end of myself, to a place where I no longer had any strength, and I finally gave up. I prayed, "Lord, help me open this door and face what is in this closet with Your power and strength."

If we look at the example of how Jesus treated His enemies, we understand how the mind of God thinks and what is in His heart. Jesus was mocked, scoffed at, criticized, and the religious leaders hated Him and plotted to kill Him. He was totally innocent and never did one wrong act. Yet He had a lot of enemies. When He was arrested, beaten, flogged, and tortured, He never spoke a word. He was nailed to a cross and punished for crimes He did not commit. He was totally innocent of any sin or evil, and as He hung there dying, He thought of all the people who had sinned against Him, and He prayed, "Father, forgive them for they know not what they do" (Luke 23:34, NIV). Jesus is the only one who can love and forgive like that.

Make no mistake, they would still be judged out of the Father's book in heaven and have to give an account for all their sins. If they remained unrepentant and unbelieving, there would be no "red-out," no blood covering them and turning the pages white again. For every debt, God would require payment in full.

"Be sure of this: The wicked will not go unpunished, but those who are righteous will go free" (Proverbs 11:21, NIV).

Jesus ascended to heaven to sit at the Father's right hand; He is exalted on high and given a name that is above all names. He has been given all authority in heaven and on Earth because He was without sin; all the pages of the Father's book in heaven were white and flawless. On Earth, He offered His forgiveness to everyone for every sin against Him. He made His blood available to anyone who would call on His name, repent, and receive Him into their hearts.

God is not asking us to forgive but to be willing to let Him work forgiveness in our hearts by His Spirit, His *supernatural* power.

You may think it's impossible to ask Jesus to apply His blood to some of the pages of your book. Only the Lord can give us the grace and power to even be willing to ask Him to do this. It may be unthinkable to you right now when everything inside you is screaming that those sins must be paid for, that the people need to be punished for them.

We can refuse to let Him erase those sins from our book, but then the Lord will be unable to erase and apply His "red-out" to our sins.

I can promise you that the Lord is able to heal and take away all the pain and trauma of those memories and events if you let Him, because He has gloriously done this in my life.

If I can be honest, one of the people who I did not think I could forgive was me. This might be the case for you too. The glorious news is that Jesus gave me the power to forgive myself too. Jesus can redeem, restore, heal, and deliver you no matter what happened or what the circumstances are. He is faithful no matter how broken or damaged the story, and He can heal a broken heart no matter how long it has been shattered. This is what He did for me.

"...where the Spirit of the Lord is, there is freedom" (2 Corinthians 3:17, NIV).

"So if the Son sets you free, you will be free indeed" (John 8:36, NIV).

The beginning of the journey to healing and freedom always starts with a prayer.

I want to share a prayer with you, but maybe you cannot pray this prayer that I have written out right now, and that is okay. You can talk to the Lord any way you desire. He is listening, and He has the power and desire to meet you wherever you are.

Dear Lord,

Kneeling before You right now, I ask You to make me whole. I confess that Jesus is the Son of God, and I ask You to be Lord of my life. Come into my broken heart. Take Your precious blood and wash me and make me white as snow. Remove all the records of my offenses against You that You have written in Your book. Surely, Jesus, You have suffered unthinkable pain and abuse in order to make Your blood available to me. I pray for the courage and grace to be willing to let You come into the hidden places in my heart that are marked "Do not enter." Lord, flood these places with the healing power of Your love. Let Your Holy Spirit's power work a miracle and give me the ability to forgive all my enemies. Let Your blood drip down on the pages of my record book and blot out all the sins written there. Make the pages of my book white and clean. Amen.

Chapter 2

CHRIST, THE INNOCENT ONE

Are you going through something in your life that seems cruel, senseless, and undeserved?

Has something happened to make you question everything you thought you knew about God?

The cross was the most heinous example of ruthless, senseless, undeserved, extreme violence ever unleashed because it was done to the holy, pure, and innocent Son of Man, Jesus Christ. To all the people watching Jesus' suffering and death on the cross, it looked like complete injustice, unthinkable cruelty, and complete abandonment from God the Father. It looked like a total victory for Satan.

The crucifixion seemed like a complete contradiction of everything Jesus said about God, His Father. Jesus taught about how much God loves us and how faithful He is to all His promises. Jesus preached about the sovereignty of God and His eternal kingdom that can never be destroyed. He spoke with authority and demonstrated His mighty power over all the power of the devil. He spoke about the Father's plan to rescue and save all

His children, give them new life, and set them free from Satan's power. Christ shared that we would rule and reign with Him in God's new kingdom.

How could all this possibly be accomplished through the cross?

The cross of Christ is truly a great mystery.

"Christ sent me . . . to preach the gospel not with words of human wisdom, lest the Cross of Christ be emptied of its power" (1 Corinthians 1:17, NIV).

Because His ways are always so much higher than our ways and His plan for accomplishing them are far beyond our capacity to comprehend, we will never understand the cross with our mind and intellect.

"For since in the wisdom of God the world through its wisdom did not know him, God was pleased through the foolishness of what was preached to save those that believe" (1 Corinthians 1:21, NIV).

God's plan was to work out His powerful redemptive purpose, which would impact the lives of everyone for eternity. He knew exactly what was happening, and He worked out every detail of it to accomplish exactly what He wanted.

Do you believe that He is the same God Almighty today in your life and circumstances?

Do you think He is a big enough God to work through every detail to accomplish something of eternal value and worth in your life?

The crucifixion must be seen through the eyes of faith, and likewise so must the trials and suffering that you are going through right now. Jesus' suffering and death was the only way for God's great salvation to come to us, set us free from the bondage and control of Satan, and make us a new creation in Christ. Everything in our lives must be viewed through these same spiritual lenses. We must believe that God is working the same way in all trials, injustice, cruelty, senseless violence, and attacks against us today by the enemy.

Through the eyes of faith, we must cling to and hold on to this wisdom, believing that He has the power to save, redeem, renew, and restore life, even when everything around us looks hopeless, and we only see destruction and death.

Everywhere Jesus went during His brief earthly ministry, everyone followed Him to listen to every word He spoke. They believed that He spoke the truth, and many came to believe He was the Messiah. So many of them had come to Him in such desperate need with all their burdens and bondage, all their pain and diseases, and He healed them and worked miracles among them. Now, how could He have died on the cross?

They must have been so confused and felt such despair. Many must have thought, *How could this possibly have happened to Jesus the Messiah?* It was incomprehensible. How could His followers get their minds around these events? They could not imagine what was being accomplished in the spirit realm and all the unseen things happening during the next three days.

"He was put to death in the body but made alive in the Spirit. In the Spirit He went and made proclamation to the imprisoned spirits—to those who were disobedient long ago when God waited patiently in the days of Noah while the ark was being made" (1 Peter 3:18, NIV).

Jesus established His complete authority over the devil and stripped him of all power. This effectively established His kingdom and reconciled everything back to the Father.

"And having disarmed the powers and authorities, he made a public spectacle of them, triumphing over them by the cross" (Colossians 2:15, NIV).

"…in putting everything under Him, God left nothing that is not subject to Him" (Hebrews 2:8, NIV).

For the followers of Jesus, the only things they were experiencing were the sights, sounds, and smell of death. Not just the death of Jesus but of all their hopes and dreams, all the promises of God that Jesus had given them. All this died with Him that day.

The spirit realm was hidden from their natural eyes; no one saw anything at Calvary except three men moaning and gasping for every breath in pain as they hung on a cross, the blood running down onto the ground underneath them. Then silence, and Jesus' lifeless body was carried to the empty tomb. Women were weeping and men were shouting. So much was being accomplished and much victory was being achieved in the unseen heavenly realms.

The same unseen realm is where the Lord is powerfully at work today. We do not get to see any of the spiritual battles or how much is being accomplished because it cannot be viewed with our human eyes.

We will never know what the followers of Jesus who witnessed His death were struggling with in their minds, what the enemy was whispering to them. Was the devil telling them:

Who will ever believe in Jesus?

How could God let such a horrible thing happen to His own Son?

God is not loving; His promises are not true.

These are the same things he whispers to us today when we are in a dark, hopeless place, when it looks like we have been abandoned or forsaken by God. We hear them echo when we feel we have been left to suffer and die. Satan uses the same tactics on all God's children that he used over 2,000 years ago.

When Jesus was crucified on the cross, it was a real challenge for His followers to witness this event and still trust and believe that God is loving, good, just, perfect, all-powerful, and in complete control. At that time, they only had their human strength and whatever measure of faith they had from the time spent with Jesus. The Holy Spirit had not yet been sent to indwell them and empower them to understand and see what was happening in the spirit world. They had no knowledge of the bigger picture and the eternal plans and purposes of God.

They did not have the New Testament and all the understanding of what was happening through this event.

The followers of Jesus were not the only witnesses present at the crucifixion. Also present were the people who Satan used to accomplish his hideous, evil plan against Christ, God's Son. They were the angry mob that was so sure that they had this event all figured out. They were sure they were right and even doing God a favor by getting rid of this "blasphemer."

"Those who passed by hurled insults at him, shaking their heads and saying, 'So! You who are going to destroy the temple and build it in three days, . . . save yourself!'" (Mark 15:29, NIV).

They also said, ". . . come down from the cross, if you are the Son of God!" (Matthew 27:40, NIV).

As they were speaking these very words, the Old Covenant was being replaced with the New Covenant of forgiveness for sins through the shed blood of Christ. The veil was torn in two in the temple in Jerusalem, making a way for all to enter into relationship with God through the righteousness and sacrifice of Jesus on the cross.

"...we have been made holy through the sacrifice of the body of Jesus Christ once for all" (Hebrews 10:10, NIV).

Scripture tells us in Mark 15:31-32, "In the same way the chief priests and the teachers of the law mocked him among themselves. 'He saved others,' they said, 'but he can't save himself'" (NIV).

They were trying to tempt Him to show His mighty power against His enemies in this evil attack. Why would He have to suffer if He were really the Son of God? They believed that if He was truly the holy and innocent Son of God, then the Father would stop this injustice.

These evil men further said, "He trusts in God. Let God rescue him now if he wants him, for he said, 'I am the Son of God'" (Matthew 27:43, NIV).

They were so deceived and so wrong in their thinking. The chief priests and scribes and teachers of the law thought they had proof now that Jesus was a liar and that He was a weak and powerless man. However, the crucifixion was the greatest and most powerful display of the strength and authority of Jesus. This power included laying down His life and being obedient to endure all the evil attacks perpetrated on His body, soul, and spirit. He took on all the sins of every man who ever lived, from Adam right down to us today, and further to everyone yet to be born in the future.

These men never realized that this event was—still is and always will be—the greatest demonstration of God's love and mercy. How hard it is for us to understand or grasp the mind of God, how He thinks and the reason behind all that happens here on this little planet called Earth.

If Jesus had listened to the crowd and intervened with His divine power to come down from the cross to destroy all the evil people who had done this to Him, He would have shown everyone His supernatural power and divine authority as the Son of God. He would have proven His innocence to the whole world. If He had done this, He would have remained everything He is and ever will be, and there would have been no penalty or loss for Him. He would have returned to the throne of God in heaven and reigned with the Father and the Holy Spirit forever.

However, the cost of sin would then have been paid by every man, woman, and child on Earth, and they would have been sentenced to a life of slavery and bondage to Satan. Everyone would have been charged the price for all their sins; payment required in full. Everyone would be charged guilty and sent to hell without hope in this life and no hope of ever seeing heaven.

Please realize: *Jesus chose to save us* instead of Himself!

Jesus went through suffering, crucifixion, and death as the Lamb slain for the atonement for our sins. He chose to pay the price in full for salvation and purchase our freedom from our sins, death, and hell. This was the purpose and plan of God the Father. It was not about how powerful God is but how much He loves us. He chose to show His love, even to all those evil people who took part in Satan's plot to kill Him. This included all the religious leaders, teachers of the law, and angry mobsters who were responsible for His death.

Jesus shed His blood for all His enemies present there that day. He prayed and asked the Father to forgive them for what they were doing to Him. Because of God the Father's immeasurable love and grace, even they were all given a way of escape through repentance and belief in Jesus.

There is only one Savior: Jesus Christ, the Son of God. He went through this path of suffering and death, and He has clearly told us that if we follow Him, we too will have to lay down our lives for others.

"To this you were called, because Christ suffered for you, leaving you an example, that you should follow in his steps" (1 Peter 2:21, NIV).

God clearly tells us that we will suffer in this life, and we will sometimes be the innocent one who pays a high price because of the sins of another. We live in a fallen world, a wicked world. If we are to imitate Christ, then we must allow the Holy Spirit to work in us the power to forgive all those who have sinned against us. God knows this is impossible for us, but with Him, all things are possible.

Being born again makes all of us Satan's mortal enemy. All the battles recorded in the Old Testament are about all the human enemy armies that came against the Israelites, God's children. Their enemies were always trying to defy and discredit the God of Israel. In the New Testament as the spiritual battles raged, it was all-out war against the Son of God, Jesus, and against all of God's children who received the Savior into their hearts.

Do not be deceived and think that the battle is over, that we are no longer in an all-out war with these evil powers and demonic armies. Although we suffer, we are not without power. Now we fight with spiritual weapons.

Our battles are "not against flesh and blood, but against rulers of the darkness of this world, and against spiritual forces of evil in heavenly realms" (see Ephesians 6:12). We can effectively fight with prayer and the Word of God against the enemy. God has given us the power to defeat our enemies in this unseen world. He will give victory in battle if we humble ourselves yet stand with our full armor on, which God has provided for us.

We must be surrendered and obedient to our Lord and King, to have our robes washed daily in the blood of Jesus, cleansed from all the stains of sin. We must be quick to ask for forgiveness and also quick to seek His grace and power to forgive others. In doing these things, we give the enemy no legal ground in our lives to defeat us, for we are not ignorant of his devices.

If you're struggling with circumstances you don't understand and you don't think it's humanly possible to survive, remember how the crucifixion looked to all the people watching. It was how the Father chose to glorify His Son and bring salvation to us. It was how He demonstrated His great love and mercy. Through what looked like unspeakable cruelty, injustice, and abandonment, He brought salvation. Remember, I said it cannot be understood or explained with human reasoning or intellect! We must stand in faith and trust that our Lord and Savior is working in the unseen realms to bring us through this trial and give us victory over our enemies, and He will be glorified in it. There is always the bigger picture and plan of the Father.

Let us pray together right now:

Dear Father,

We come to You and pray for the courage and faith to stand fearlessly on Your promises in Your Word. We believe that You are faithfully at work in the unseen spiritual realm bringing about another opportunity, through our impossible situation, where You will be glorified in and through our lives. Lord, Your plans will succeed, and You will accomplish all that You have purposed because we have come to You, laying all these burdens and pain at the foot of the cross, surrendering all to You. Let Your blood and Your resurrection power work forgiveness, healing, deliverance, and miracles in our lives. Amen.

Let me encourage you that I have experienced His love and power in and through many hopeless circumstances in my life. I have seen Him turn them around to bring glory to His name and new life and hope to me. He has given me beauty for ashes, restored ruins and broken places in my life, and made them new. I can come with faith, boldly and confidently, before His throne with you, asking Him to work the same miracles in your life. I believe the Lord will hear our humble cry.

Chapter 3

WORSHIP

We all know what it feels like to be with someone whom you love more than life. It almost feels euphoric. It is exhilarating, and there is this sense of wholeness and wellness throughout your whole being. This is what true worship feels like, and it is what the Lord created us to experience with Him.

True worship is not an activity, something we do at church, or just a name for the part of the service where we are singing and playing music to prepare for entering into a time of fellowship with the Lord. Our whole relationship with the Lord is worship. It is such a rich, dynamic word full of passion and meaning.

"To love the Lord with all our heart and mind and soul and strength" (see Luke 10:27).

Worship is an expression of love.

The Lord created us with this passion and desire deep in our hearts so that it would be possible for everyone to have a meaningful and passionate relationship with Him.

Worship is in our blood, our DNA. We do it all day long every day mostly without thought or even being aware of it. We are hardwired to worship God and enjoy His presence. It is the outward expression of our love for Him.

In a thesaurus, the word "worship" may also direct you to words like these: adoration, devotion, praise, to honor, to lift up and glorify, to celebrate; to devote time, resources, and love to. With these explanations of the word "worship," I think about my life, and there is a constant song of worship that is heard in everything I speak about and everything I do. God also gave us a free will so we can choose to worship Him out of love, because He wants us to be motivated by love and not fear of Him. He makes this possible through the power of His Spirit.

Our lives are a journey. This journey should lead us to the Lord of love and into an undivided relationship with Him where He is the one to whom we are devoted 100 percent of the time. Worship is a gift that the Lord plants deep in our heart and then lets it develop and grow over time.

In our natural lives, we start out as worshipers of self. As our little world expands, we worship and adore our parents, toys, comforts, and pleasures. Then we are introduced to the fun of many other things, such as sports, games, movies, entertainment, social interactions, and music.

When we are in our teenage and young-adulthood years, we focus extra attention on our outward appearance, how others see us, and what they think. We devote time, money, and energy into looking good. We devote ourselves to our boyfriend/girlfriend with wholehearted abandonment. We pursue education, careers, and success in this world. Marriage—someone to adore, love, and share our lives with—is also part of the plans we have for ourselves and our future. These are all good things. These were all created by our loving Father to bless us.

However, we also have an enemy, Satan, and he has plans to use all these good things to draw us away from wholehearted devotion to the Lord. He does not want us to experience this passionate and deep relationship with the Lord because we will become a real threat to him. It will make it extremely hard for him to succeed in his schemes to destroy us. He does not just use evil to get us to worship other things instead of the Lord. No matter if you were born into a Christian family or into an ungodly family, the plans and schemes of the enemy are to teach us to direct our worship toward self and creation, away from the Creator. Satan knows we are created to be worshipers. He cannot change that fact; he knows we are passionately driven and made to love and devote ourselves in worship to God alone, with all our heart, soul, mind, and strength.

There is another dimension of worship, and God's reason for creating so much in this world to enjoy. His purpose was not to make it harder for us to worship Him. God has a heart that is full of love and His desire is to share everything in all creation with us, and then for us to have such an abundance that we will be able to pass it along and bless others. This is also part of the way in which we worship and give glory to the Lord.

Paul says, "Command them to do good, be rich in good deeds, and to be generous and willing to share. In this way they will lay up treasures for themselves as a firm foundation for the coming age, so that they may take hold of the life that is truly life" (1 Timothy 6:18-19, NIV).

This "life that is truly life" is the intimate relationship with the Lord Himself. The Lord gives us blessings and gifts to enjoy and to share with others. When we start to worship or see these gifts as earned, thinking that they belong to us, it is very difficult to share them with others.

Pride and self-centeredness are part of our carnal nature. This is the part that can be open to the enemy's whispers when he says things like, *You've worked so hard for what you have, and sacrificed so much, why should you share with someone else who hasn't earned it?*

Do you hear that spirit of arrogance and pride in these thoughts? We have forgotten that we brought nothing into this world and we will take nothing out; our very next breath is a gift from God. Everything that we have has been freely given by God: a mind that can think clearly, ears that can hear and understand the words of God, a heart that can know Him, eyes that can see, a voice that can speak, arms and legs that can move. What an amazing human body that can function, one fearfully and wonderfully made by God! There is nothing that we have done to deserve these gifts.

We can find safety from the enemy's snares if we are careful to remember how uncertain and temporary our possessions are. Be careful that nothing starts to creep in to take His place. We express trust in God, His faithfulness, and His love for us by giving away what He has given to us in the first place and sharing with those who do not deserve it, just like we did not deserve it.

God has shown me that everything is temporary and has an expiration date. They are gifts given for enjoyment to bless me for a season.

If I go for a walk in the fall and look at the grass, flowers, and turning leaves, I have enjoyed them for a season, but now their temporary life is ending. When I go to the grocery store, everything I buy has an expiration date. I do not challenge this; I am intelligent enough to know that these are perishable goods. I eat and enjoy them until the date comes up.

This is a daily reminder that everything in my life has only been given for a time and season. All the people whom I love and have relationships with are also gifts that the Lord has given for a season. Each one of us has been given an exact number of days by our Creator. He planned and purposed them before we were born.

"Your eyes saw my unformed body, all the days ordained for me were written in your book before one of them came to be" (Psalm 139:16, NIV).

Evil and all of the demonic hosts, and even Satan himself, have an expiration date too. The Lord will bring to an end all their activity, pain, suffering, violence, and destruction. All of Satan's kingdom will be completely annihilated and there will be no trace of it, or even a single memory left of it (see Isaiah 65:17).

With all this overwhelming evidence of how short and fleeting all of life is, there is such a temptation to cling too tightly to the things of this world. Jesus said, "If anyone comes to me and does not hate father and mother, wife and children, brothers and sisters—yes, even their own life—such a person cannot be my disciple. And whoever does not carry their cross and follow me cannot be my disciple" (Luke 14:26-27, NIV).

The Lord speaks throughout all His creation a clear message that comes from His loving heart. He warns us and shows how temporary everything here on Earth really is. His motivation is so we will not turn to these things and fall into the deadly traps and temptations that the enemy has set all along our path.

Each day I awake to one more day that God has given me. I want to give all my praise, worship, adoration to the Lord who loves me with all His heart and soul, as He tells me in His Word: "I will inspire them to fear Me, so that they never turn away from Me, I will rejoice in doing them good and will assuredly plant them in this land with all My heart and soul" (Jeremiah 32:40, NIV).

He is ready to accomplish everything in my life He desires. The Lord alone is the source of eternal strength and power; He provides everything we need. Jesus is the only One who satisfies the deep longings that are in our hearts, not just temporarily, but permanently and forever. To worship anything or anyone besides God is idolatry and spiritual harlotry. These things may produce the same euphoria and rich pleasurable feeling, but they are never lasting and lead us onto a path away from God and into darkness.

Scripture says to not trust in uncertain riches, or anything in the world that we are tempted to worship more than "the living God, who gives us richly all things to enjoy" (1 Timothy 6:17, KJV). The very things that were all meant to draw us closer to Him can become the very things that distract and draw us away. We must not become presumptuous about anything, as if all that we have are not gifts from God.

"For from him and through Him and for Him are all things. To him be the glory forever! Amen" (Romans 11:36, NIV).

There was a time in my life when my relationship with the Lord was growing and good. Then I found myself working extremely hard, starting to accomplish some pretty amazing things, and believing that somehow I deserved the success. I got my eyes off the Lord and onto myself. The enemy has so many ways to get us off track and into idolatry. This detour that he led me onto was a very dark and rough road. It led to a fall and a lot of pain and regrets.

However, the Lord was faithful to rescue and bring me back onto the right path, restoring me into relationship with Him once again. Because of this time of trial, I learned to be more alert and guard my heart. It made me appreciate and cherish my relationship with Him more. What Satan meant for evil, God used for good.

Are you struggling with idolatry? Is there something or someone who has replaced God in your heart, something that you do not think you can live without? Satan knows how weak and vulnerable we are to the things of this life and this world. He takes full advantage of this fact. Though it is a harder thing to know God and His presence, it is by no means impossible. In fact it is God's perfect will and plan for us. God has brought me into this very relationship with Him, even after all my unfaithfulness to Him.

There is a story in the Bible in the book of Hosea about idolatry that explains God's heart on this subject.

Hosea was a high priest and righteous servant of God. As a prophet of his day, Hosea was asked by God to perform a difficult and humiliating task. He was to defile himself by breaking the Jewish law and marry a prostitute named Gomer. He also knew that she would continue to have other lovers and be unfaithful. At this time, the nation of Israel had slipped into idolatry. The Lord instructed Hosea, "When the LORD began to speak through Hosea, the LORD said to him, 'Go, marry a promiscuous woman and have children with her, for like an adulterous wife this land is guilty of unfaithfulness to the LORD'" (Hosea 1:2, NIV).

Gomer's adulterous living would be a vivid illustration of Israel's unfaithfulness in their covenant relationship with the Lord. This marriage was doomed for disaster before the vows were even spoken. What trust and obedience it took on Hosea's part to go through with this plan and allow God to use him in this way. Because of Gomer's adulteries and running after other lovers, the marriage soon disintegrated, and she eventually became the concubine and slave of another man. The Lord did not let Gomer remain in slavery. The Lord then instructed Hosea to go and buy her back, to redeem and restore her into relationship again.

This becomes true for us when we begin to worship anything outside of God. Hosea's role was to show the idolatry and the dark path that the children of God were on and where it would lead if they didn't turn back to God. The Lord's plan was for Hosea to pay the price for her sins and take Gomer back, to love and care for her in a covenant marriage relationship. The Lord is showing us just how wicked our hearts can be and how easily we are tempted to seek out and love someone or something that will never satisfy and will only lead to bondage, pain, and suffering, just like Hosea's wife.

Jesus has made a covenant and promise that He will sanctify and cleanse His church (His Bride) with the washing of the Word. He desires to present her to Himself a glorious church, not having spot or wrinkle or any such thing, but that we should be holy and without blemish (see Ephesians 5:26-27). This is His plan and He has the power to work this into our lives, no matter how far we wander away or how much idolatry we have fallen into. This account of Hosea and Gomer is so full of hope.

Worship to God is the type of relationship we were created for. I have talked about what worship looks like and the ways the enemy can distract and deceive us away from worshiping the Lord. My prayer for you is that you know and experience this amazing unconditional and endless love that the Lord has for you. I pray that you will have no doubt about this truth and that the Holy Spirit will minister to your heart. I pray He will also fill you with hope, courage, and strength to turn back to the Lord with all your heart and fall into His waiting open arms.

I hope that you will be encouraged by this message of hope.

He has the power to redeem and restore your relationship from wherever you are. Maybe right now you are not trapped in a snare that has taken you down a road far from the path you were on with the Lord. Maybe this message will be an encouragement and help to keep you from being distracted or deceived at some fork in the road ahead.

The Lord has told us in the book of Ephesians to speak to each other in psalms and hymns and spiritual songs every day. These are all words from the Lord that are to instruct us and keep us on the right path. If you are someone who has found yourself caught in a trap and hopelessly imprisoned in bondage with no way to purchase your freedom again, like Gomer, I have the best news ever! Jesus has paid the price in full with His blood for you, and He wants to rescue you and restore you to relationship with

Him today. He has created you to belong to Him and to worship Him so you can find everything that you ever wanted or needed in Him.

Chapter 4

INCENSE AND PRAYERS

Do you long for a closer, more real relationship with the Lord?

Are you wondering how that happens, and is it really possible?

We are in Christ and Christ is in us. Part of the amazing reality of this is that when we are in the Word, and the Word is in our hearts, we can be in fellowship with God all the time. The Word is alive and full of power. The more we are in the Word, the more we can experience this living, real relationship with Jesus. There should be nothing more important in the life of a believer than prayer and reading the Word. We learn to know and understand the Lord through reading His Word, and He hears and listens to what we have to say through our prayers. He uses prayer as the vehicle with which to bring about His plans and purpose, to battle His enemies, and to bring His kingdom to Earth as it is in heaven.

Wow! That is amazing and hard for me to get my mind around.

In heaven the Creator of the whole universe, the Lord of lords and King of kings, the almighty God, desires an active and meaningful relationship with a weak and selfish creature like me.

From before time, the Lord has had a passion for fellowship and relationship with man. He was the originator of the relationship and He created the covenant with us, vowing His eternal love and faithfulness to us.

All the books and chapters in the Bible are filled with accounts of God's unfailing commitment and faithfulness, no matter how many times His children rebelled, rejected Him, and turned away from Him. His passion for us never grows weak, and He never gives up on us. His love has no limits and no borders.

When I was a child, my father was a strong and self-controlled man. He was hard-working and held down two (and sometimes three) jobs to support our family. However, this meant he was unavailable to be an active supporter or someone for me to turn to.

When I became a Christian, and for many years after, I thought that God was a strong and busy heavenly Father, that He had more serious things to deal with than my wants and needs. I did not want to bother Him.

I knew He was committed to taking care of me, but I did not think He wanted to really know me or have a deep, personal relationship with me. I pictured Him up in heaven with all the jobs of running the world, heaven, and everything in everyone else's life and being too busy for me.

As I studied the Bible, I began to see that my heavenly Father was not anything like what I imagined Him to be. The Holy Spirit started to open the Scriptures up to me. I started to see how loving, compassionate, and personal He is. He longs to hear from me, to have me sit and talk to Him, and to tell Him everything that is on my heart. Our relationship has grown and deepened, and when I spend time with Him, we talk about what is on His heart too.

Through prayer, we speak and listen to each other about everything, and the time spent with Him is my greatest joy now. It is alive and as real as any human relationship and is actually deeper and more satisfying. This is His plan for every one of us.

Countless books have been written on the subject of prayer. Here is a personal perspective that I have encountered.

As I have sought the Lord for more understanding from heaven's viewpoint, this is some of what the Lord has revealed to me as to what our prayers look like when they arrive in heaven before God's throne.

Of course, there are millions of prayers arriving every second, and as mere mortals, it is hard for us to imagine this. The Lord devotes His undivided attention to every one of our prayers when it arrives. The Lord is outside of time and space, and He is not limited by them. He is God, and He can listen and share His time with us, just as if we were the only one talking. That is amazing enough, but then the Scriptures tell us that He records everything. While we are talking to Him, He is also making sure that not one word we speak is lost or forgotten.

What person on Earth would write down everything we say, not forgetting one word?

That is out of this world! Nobody loves like that. Do not think for a minute that the only prayers God hears and records are the ones we pray in church or when we are full of faith and boldness. He even hears the prayers from the depth of despair, when we can only cry out loud to God about the pain, even the groans no words can describe. The Spirit of God can hear and understand what is in our heart, and when the wordless sounds arrive in heaven, God hears and understands our heart's cries.

I pray the Lord will give you revelation knowledge of these truths so that you can see the Lord in heaven more clearly.

The Bible says, "You keep track of all my sorrows. You have collected all my tears in your bottle. You have recorded each one in your book" (Psalm 56:8). The Lord not only stores and preserves our tears in a bottle in heaven, but He records when they were shed, the reason why, and, just like our prayers, they are kept by Him to be brought out in His perfect time. All the pain, sorrow, and suffering that caused those tears to fall will be erased. God saw them fall from your eyes, and He was there to collect them so that not one fell to the ground.

Jesus shared a deep and real relationship with His disciples and followers, and His devotion to them displayed the passion and heart of the Father for relationship. He called them "friends" and laid down His life for them. He promised that every believer could and would have a personal and real relationship with Him and the Father. "And I will ask the Father, and he will give you another advocate to help you and be with you forever—the Spirit of truth. The world cannot accept him, because it neither sees him nor knows him. But you know him, for he lives with you and will be in you" (John 14:16-17, NIV).

"But the Advocate, the Holy Spirit, whom the Father will send in my name, will teach you all things and will remind you of everything I have said to you" (John 14:26, NIV).

Even Abraham and Moses never knew God with His Spirit dwelling in their hearts. This new covenant relationship with believers was the indwelling of the Spirit of God in our spirit. This was the heart of God all along: to not just live with us but also to live in us.

As I was studying in Revelation, the Lord gave me some deeper insight into what our prayers look like when they get to heaven. "Another angel, who had a golden censer, came and stood at the altar. He was given much incense to offer, with the prayers of all God's people, on the golden altar in front of the throne. The smoke of the incense, together with the prayers of God's people, went up before God from the angel's hand" (8:3-4, NIV).

When I read this verse, I can picture the angel dressed in bright, glowing robes and carrying in his hands the censer and prayers. Some prayers are transformed into sharp swords and arrows. These would be dispatched directly to the front line into spiritual battles raging in the heavenly realms against Satan and his armies.

Somewhere in heaven, the Lord is recording all our prayers. Can you imagine? Our prayers are put into some tangible form and gathered. We are also told that our prayers have an aroma and fragrance in heaven, a sweet, soothing aroma that the Lord can smell, as the angels bring our prayers before Him. In this world, everything has a fragrance or aroma. Science has discovered that the sense of smell is more closely linked to memory than any of our other senses. It plays a very important role in mood and emotions as well.

There are many references to the aroma of offering and sacrifices that the priests of the Old Testament brought and put on the altar to the Lord. The Lord mentions the "soothing aroma" of Noah's sacrifice of burnt offering after the flood: "The Lord smelled the pleasing aroma and said in his heart: 'Never again will I curse the ground because of humans'"(Genesis 8:21, NIV). Noah's heartfelt devotion and prayers were received by God as a sweet and pleasing aroma.

As a child, I prayed a lot to Jesus and believed that He both heard and would answer. I prayed about small things and big things, years of prayers. Do you remember some of your childhood prayers to the Lord? Most of the prayers, I do not remember at all. Even the prayers that I prayed while going through severe trials, I fail to remember. Yet my loving Father considers each one so important that He not only listens but also makes sure that they are written down. Not one will go unanswered, and not one will be forgotten. That is beyond amazing to me—that the Lord recorded every word I spoke, and they were transformed into something tangible that the angels are carrying around in bowls in their hands.

In the temple of the Old Testament, the Lord had a professional perfumer making incense and oil for Him so that He could enjoy the smell of it when the sacrifices and offerings were made. "They also made the sacred anointing oil and the pure, fragrant incense—the work of a perfumer" (Exodus 37:29, NIV). Incense was a mixture of pulverized aromatic gum resins and frankincense, which was salted to produce a visible cloud of sweet-smelling smoke.

It was burned as a regular sacrifice at sunrise and sunset on the gold-plated altar standing before the Most Holy Place (see Exodus 30:7-8). This is the shadow of the Most Holy Place of God in heaven. Only the aromatic cloud could penetrate and go through the veil, or curtain, that sealed off the divine presence of God. The priests were not allowed to go in. As they offered the incense with the prayers for the people's sins, and worshiped God, it was an act of devotion.

Because of Christ's crucifixion, "the curtain of the temple was torn in two from top to bottom" (Matthew 27:51), and our prayers can now be taken right into the holy of holies to the throne of God in heaven. The cloud of smoke from the incense with our prayers goes up to God and creates a tangible substance and fragrance.

What our prayers look like when they reach heaven is amazing. When I send up my prayers to Him, all my words are carried straight into His presence. They are heard and seen, and the Lord smells the accompanying sweet aroma of them. "May my prayers be set before you like incense; may the lifting up of my hands be like an evening sacrifice" (Psalm 141:2, NIV). God is the Creator of fragrance and all the aromas that come from everything in heaven and on Earth. It is for His pleasure that they are created, and I believe that the aroma is sweet as the prayers come up before Him. The aroma of our prayers touches the mind and heart of the Lord.

Revelation 5:8-9 speaks of a day in the future at the end of the ages: on that day, the Lamb will take the scroll from the Father's right hand, "And when he had taken it, the four living creatures and the twenty-four elders fell down before the Lamb. Each one had a harp [to accompany singing] and they were holding golden bowls full of incense, which are the prayers of God's people. And they sang a new song" (NIV).

With this new insight, I have even more desire to spend time with Him, to offer up my prayers just like fragrant incense that will bless Him, and to listen as He speaks through His Word to me. I hope that it will also encourage you so that you may have a new vision of the Father's love. I also pray that you would see that the desire of His heart is to be in relationship with you in a real and personal way. May you see your prayers as something tangible and touchable in heaven and see the Father listening, making sure that every word is recorded and held close to His heart.

I also hope you would see the immediate attention and orchestration of every detail for your answer. The prayers that are not for your best and do not fit into the bigger and better plans that He has for you are answered with a no. But even when this happens, they are still given the same careful attention. And if you seek Him and humble yourself, spending time with Him, He can give you wisdom and revelation as to the reason He answered such, or the grace to live with the questions until the answer comes.

My prayer is that the Lord will quicken His scriptures that have been spoken and used in this letter to you. I hope that you would be encouraged and strengthened by His Spirit to seek the Lord, to pray, and to talk to Him about everything, to see prayer as real fellowship with a Father who loves you and is listening to every word, and even every groan and cry. He wants you to share everything with Him and to trust and believe Him for the best and perfect answers for each one.

Chapter 5

HEALING THE LAME BEGGAR

In the Bible, Acts 3:1-10 tells us about an encounter that the disciples had that was amazing. One day Peter and John were going up to the temple at the time of prayer; it was three in the afternoon. "Now a man crippled from birth was being carried to the temple gate called Beautiful where he was put every day to beg from those going into the temple courts" (v. 3).

When the beggar saw Peter and John about to enter, he asked them for money. He lay crippled on a mat with no strength in his feet or ankles. He was unable to go into the temple courts and worship God like everyone else. Every day he had to watch as the people walked past him, making their way to the temple.

How he must have longed to see the inside, to listen to the teachers of the Law reading out of the written holy books, and to hear the psalms sung and the glorious worship. His life was to watch others going into the temple where they enjoyed being in the presence of God and worshiping, offering sacrifices, and fellowshipping with each other.

Many were dressed in nice clothes and had happy faces; the Lord had blessed them with prosperity and health. They were free from crippling disease, free to walk and work, free to accomplish whatever they had on their hearts to do.

The place where he lay on his mat was the temple gate called Beautiful, but there was nothing beautiful about his life. He had been crippled from birth. During his lifetime, he had never experienced the blessings that all these people passing by him enjoyed every day. Growing up as a child, he would have only sat and watched other children play, run, climb trees, swim in the river, and do all the fun things that children do. He never experienced the fellowship and friendships they enjoyed as they shared adventures together. For years, he only watched others do all the things he could not do.

Then the glorious day came when Peter and John walked by, looked straight at him, and Peter said to him, "Look at us!" The man gave them his full attention with expectation that he was going to receive something. This beggar was told to take his eyes off everything around him and everything that he was doing. Then Peter said, "Silver or gold I do not have, but what I do have I give you. In the name of Jesus Christ of Nazareth, walk" (Acts 3:6, NIV).

If Peter had gold and silver to offer, what a limited use it would have been to this lame man. Maybe he could have bought a better mat to sit on or maybe warmer clothes.

If Peter had given the man enough money so that he never had to beg again—money to have a home, food, friends who respected him and didn't look down on him—even worldly good things would not change the fact that he was still lame and unable to walk.

How much greater the gift and blessing that God had planned for him. It was so far beyond material possessions or worldly honor and position. Being lame also classified him as "unclean" according to Jewish Law, disqualifying him from entering the temple and rendering him rejected by God.

Peter commanded him to walk and took him by the right hand. As Peter helped him up, the man's feet and ankles instantly became strong.

"He jumped to his feet and began to walk. Then he went with them into the temple courts, walking and jumping, and praising God" (Acts 3:8, NIV).

After all the days, weeks, months, and years when he watched everyone else walk into the temple to worship God—while he sat outside on his mat, living with hopelessness and shame—at last he was set free. Instantly, he was changed and entered into a new life with the Lord.

"When all the people saw him walking and praising God, they recognized him as the same man who used to sit begging at the temple gate called Beautiful, and they were filled with wonder and amazement at what had happened to him" (vv 9-10).

This could have been the first time in his whole life that this man got to see the inside of the temple; he was no longer considered "unclean." God had poured out His love on him, healing and honoring him above everyone else who was there. That day, this beggar was exonerated, shown respect, and made whole in his body. This was the first day in his life that he felt acceptance and enjoyed the respect of all the people there; even the priests and rulers, elders and teachers took notice of him.

How amazing it must have been for him. After all his suffering and pain, he was rewarded. This man received healing in his life here on Earth, but I can assure you that the Lord has promised that we will all be rewarded. He will make up for everything that we have endured and suffered in this world. For some of us, it will be in heaven, but make no mistake, the Lord is always faithful. He will reward every one of us in a greater and unimaginable way.

We are promised that our suffering will not compare to the glory that will be revealed: "I consider that our present sufferings are not worthy compared to the glory that will be revealed in us" (Romans 8:18, NIV). Many times the wait for this glory to be seen is painfully long and lonely. To persevere and endure takes all the faith we have, trusting year after year.

How many times had Peter and John taken this road to the temple and passed by this beggar sitting on his mat?

How many times had Jesus and the disciples gone to Jerusalem to worship at the temple and celebrate the feast days?

Did they walk past him too?

He had been there every day for years. There would have been days in the past when they would have seen him, yet passed by. God had an appointed time, an exact hour, day, month, and year, when He chose to touch this lame beggar. We do not know why the Lord chose this specific day, but I know that everything that the Lord does has a specific, divine purpose and also perfectly ordained time. God sent His Son at the perfect time: "You see, at just the right time, when we were still powerless, Christ died for the ungodly" (Romans 5:6, NIV).

Christ will also return at the perfect time: "But about that day or hour no one knows, not even the angels in heaven, nor the Son, but only the Father" (Matthew 24:36, NIV).

In Revelation, John talks about the judgment and angels that will be sent to Earth. He said, "And the four angels who had been kept ready for this very hour and day and month and year were released to kill a third of mankind" (Revelation 9:15).

This verse should give us assurance that God is exact and precise about everything He does. This is part of His amazing and unchanging character.

The most familiar verses about God's perfect time are in Ecclesiastes 3:1-3: "There is a time for everything, and a season for every activity under the heavens: a time to be born and a time to die, a time to plant and a time to uproot, a time to kill and a time to heal, a time to tear down and a time to build" (NIV).

Maybe you have had an illness since childhood, or maybe you have lived with something or someone for years, and you are feeling like the Lord just keeps passing you by. He surely sees you sitting there but seems to choose to walk right by you.

How can He be a loving Father and not be willing to help, to heal, or to deliver you from your circumstances right now? How much longer do you have to suffer and live like this?

I know that God has orchestrated our lives and knew all our days before we were even born (see Psalm 139:13). He is acutely aware of every detail of our lives, and His watchful eyes are always upon us.

He takes the time to count the hairs (see Luke 12:7) on our head, which seems like such a useless task and of no value. Does He do this so we will know how much He sees, knows, and cares about everything? Surely this same God cares about the trials we go through and the things we suffer, but He also knows the beginning from the end. His eternal plans are so complex and lofty that we cannot understand them at all.

"For you created my inmost being; you knit me together in my mother's womb. My frame was not hidden from you when I was made in the secret place....Your eyes saw my unformed body; all the days ordained for me were written in your book before one of them came to be" (Psalm 139:13, 15-16, NIV).

This is the Father who loves us and has our lives all planned. He has woven together a plan for our greatest good and also one for the good of many other people, whom our lives will touch someday.

God, in His sovereignty, chose this day to work a miracle for the lame beggar. His story of healing spread throughout all of Jerusalem. This one man was used by God in a mighty way to touch the lives of thousands. His story is still touching lives today and will continue to touch lives in the future. Millions of people have now heard of this miracle that the Lord did for this one man.

What a story of redemption, of God's love and grace. This man is in heaven now and able to see all the lives that were changed because of his suffering and long-awaited healing. Perhaps he now knows that it was all worth it, and he would do it again to see millions touched.

I do not know if this man was also healed of all the pain and trauma he suffered for over forty years. We know that he was physically healed the moment that Peter spoke and took his hand and he began to walk for the first time. There is no more information about this man after that.

In my life, the Lord has miraculously healed me in a moment of time, touched my heart and made me whole again in a broken or damaged area of my life. However, there have been other times—and more often—when the healing process has been slower and over time. Whether it took only an instant or it was a longer process, God was faithful to heal and make me whole in many areas. I believe in His power and love to heal, restore, and make new.

The Lord in His love and wisdom chooses how short or long the process will be, and He also chooses the method, resources, and people to use. We need to understand there is always a bigger picture and perfect plan that God has for our lives for His greatest glory. We all want the healing to be instant, right now like this lame beggar experienced. What do we do in the circumstances and areas where the Lord has asked us to wait, where we do not see the miracle we need now? The Lord has His perfect timing, and He sometimes waits until all human help has failed and hope of healing is gone because too much time has passed for healing to be possible. This is the place where God can receive the greater glory and praise for the miracle He works.

Sometimes He uses the waiting and delay to help us work through some of our thinking that does not line up with His so that He can first free us from these wrong beliefs and ideas about Him. Other times, the Lord wants to open our eyes so we can see how totally weak and powerless we are. Then we can receive the revelation and truth about our frail frame and our desperate need for His strength and power every minute of the day. These are all important lessons that build our faith and relationship with the Lord and take precedence over healing sometimes. These are only some of the reasons for the Lord's seeming delays in the answers to our prayers or the healing that we so desperately need and desire.

When I first became a Christian, and for many years after, I started out with a lot of wrong thinking. I thought that if I prayed hard, was obedient, and had faith in the Lord, He would heal and change my circumstances and the people in my life who brought me pain and suffering. I was sure He would do it right away too, but after thirty years of working and striving to help God out with these issues, I became weary and discouraged.

My faith was shaken, and I gave up. I started to take back the control of my life in regards to these areas. In my frustration, I thought that I would help God out by doing the work for Him. I was sure that if I just tried harder and was stronger, I could do it. This was a serious mistake and caused extra suffering and pain to me as well as to others. It was a detour that delayed God's plans for me for a while, but the Lord faithfully and mercifully brought me back to the right path again with Him.

I am eternally grateful that the Lord loved me enough to let me totally fail in fixing and changing things by myself.

It was humbling, but I learned to trust Him to work it out His way and in His timing in a greater way than I had ever known before. He used even my mistakes to work for good in my life. All glory to Him alone!

"For from him and through him and for him are all things. To him be the glory forever! Amen" (Romans 11:36, NIV).

The Lord's purpose and plans have to do with us becoming who He wants us to be. To accomplish this, sometimes our wants and needs have to be delayed. I know that there may be many of you who have suffered extreme and unbearable trials, and you are paralyzed by these circumstances.

You also have an enemy that is always trying to convince you that your situation is hopeless and will never change, hoping you lose heart and give up. You must hold on to the truth and the promises of God: there is an exact day and time when this will end, you will be free, and God will be glorified in your life in an amazing way.

One day you will see the purpose and that God was right there with you through it all.

One day it will make complete sense, and the reward and recompense will be galaxies above what you could have imagined or thought.

Like the old song says, "It will be worth it all when we see Jesus, Life's trials will seem so small when we see Christ; One glimpse from His dear face all sorrow will erase."

It does not mean the trials here are small; they certainly are not! It means that in heaven and in the presence of Jesus, they will be erased by one look of His loving and glorious face.

I am asking you to hold on for one more day, one more week, even one more month. Just like the beggar, hold on until the Lord's day arrives. You may not know all the reasons why there was such a long delay until you sit down with the Lord in heaven. But I know the answer will one day be clear and understandable.

For now, you need to hold on to the hope held out in Jesus, and keep your eyes fixed on Him. Just hold on a little while longer.

I believe that it was not until this man went to heaven that he saw the full extent of his miraculous life, its impact and the glory it brought to the Lord. The Lord will come at the exact and perfect time.

"Let us hold unswervingly to the hope we profess, for he who promised is faithful" (Hebrews 10:23, NIV).

Jesus sustains all things by His powerful word (see Hebrews 1:3).

And the Lord said, "God left nothing that is not subject to Him" (Hebrews 2:8, NIV).

My prayer for you is that the Lord will open up the Scriptures, speak to your heart, and minister as only His Spirit can through His powerful Word. I pray that He will speak supernaturally and give you the very scriptures that will be exactly what will give you hope, comfort, and courage you need right now.

As you cry out to the Lord in this dark night, watching for the rays of light for the day that you have been waiting for, hold on to this promise:

"Let the morning bring me word of your unfailing love, for I have put my trust in You. Show me the way I should go, for to you I entrust my life. Rescue me from my enemies, Lord, for I hide myself in you" (Psalm 143:8-9, NIV).

Chapter 6

"PETER, DO YOU LOVE ME?"

Most of us are very familiar with the conversation Jesus had with Peter about love in John 21:15-17. When Peter was questioned by Jesus concerning his love for his Savior, his consistent answer was yes. Jesus asked him three times. When we tell someone "I love you," what are we really saying? The Lord is asking all of us, "Do you really love Me?" As I examine my heart, I see a lot of my love for Jesus has selfish motives.

There is a song that I sing in church that says, "I need You, Oh, I need You, Jesus, every hour I need You, Oh bless me now my Savior, I come to Thee." There is no doubt that I desperately need Jesus every hour, every day. Jesus ministers to me spiritually, emotionally, and physically, meeting all my needs. The source is coming from His great love for me. But Jesus is not asking me, "Do you need Me?"

I am discovering that needing someone is not the same as loving them. If I were graded on these, I would surely receive an A in my need for Jesus, but in my love for Him, my grade would probably be more like a C or D. My motivation for the relationship has been more about my needs most of the time than about my love.

I start each day by getting up early in the morning, reading the Bible, and praying to the Lord, and He ministers to me. We have wonderful fellowship. I need Him and cannot live without Him. I spend much time in prayer for the needs of others. This sounds so spiritual. This is only one side of the relationship, however; the other side of the relationship is asking my Lord, "How can I bring You joy and bless You? How can I be obedient to let You lead and guide my steps today, wherever You lead me?"

The Lord is real, and He has feelings and desires. He created us to share His life and His creation with Him—not because He needed us, but because He loves us. The Father is creating a spiritual Bride for His Son, Jesus, one that will be in intimate relationship and love Him as He deserves to be loved.

To love Jesus is to let Him love others through me. I desire and seek to become part of this Bride of Christ, but I don't yet see that same depth of love in me that He is looking for or deserves. I am still a work in progress, but I believe He will faithfully complete this work in me (see Philippians 1:6).

I know with all my heart that Jesus loves me; that is the easy part. But to show my love for Him by letting Him love others through my life is the hard part. If I really love Him, then I will be willing to surrender my life and let Him show His love through me to others. I pray to the Lord, "Transform me into what You desire. Create in my heart the love for You that I lack."

In Psalm 119:33-38, David cries out for the Lord to do this transforming work in his life. He prayed to the Lord, willingly surrendering his life, knowing that it would be God who would do it all. In these scriptures, we see that God is the one who gives understanding, directs us, turns our hearts, and yes, renews our life to fulfill His promises. Like David, we all must come to the place of complete abandonment and dependency on God alone. Then this transformation will take place.

When I look at Peter and his relationship with Jesus, I understand why Jesus had to show Peter what his real heart condition was. Peter was such an amazingly gifted man. He had passion, zeal, self-control, character, and a very strong spirit. He considered himself Jesus' best friend, and he was so confident in his love for the Lord. He believed that he possessed the ability to love others like Jesus with his own strength. The truth is that if he could have mustered up all his human love, strength, gifting, and knowledge to exercise them all at one time, to fight against this "great temptation" he faced at the time of Jesus' crucifixion, it still would have been no match against the devil. Peter believed that he would never be capable of betraying Jesus. He believed this lie and strong delusion about himself. God could not and would not use him until the truth about his heart condition was exposed, seen, and dealt with. Jesus would never have been able to convince Peter of this truth about himself; he had to experience being left alone to see what would happen when he tried to love Jesus with only his own strengths and ability.

What a coveted gift and blessing it is for God to show us our true heart condition. To see how desperately wicked and deceitful it is above all things can be painful, but this is knowledge we need to receive. Peter actually thought he was capable of loving no matter what happened, as if his human love was as strong as Jesus' divine love for him. Peter even boasted that he would die for Jesus before he would disown Him.

"But Peter declared, even if I have to die with You, I will never disown You" (Matthew 26:35, NIV).

Jesus answered, "Will you really lay down your life for Me? I tell you the truth, this very night before the rooster crows, you will disown Me three times" (John 13:38, NIV). The Lord had to show Peter how weak human love is and allow Peter to fail in his own human strength.

It is interesting that Peter said he would die for Jesus because this was the very thing that Jesus was about to do on the cross. It was a very proud statement for Peter to compare his love to Christ's love. After Christ's resurrection, He appeared to the disciples, and He asked Peter, "Simon, son of John, do you love me more than these?" (John 21:15, NIV). This time, Peter was a different man with a new understanding of how limited and weak his love was. He now knew that his human love did not come close to Jesus' love.

In his limited love, Peter could have possibly loved people some of the time. However, only Jesus can love everyone all the time, even the unlovable ones—no matter how broken, evil, damaged, and lost they are. It is Jesus and His love that the world needs.

The gospel of Christ is not about how much we love Jesus, with the emphasis being on us. Peter boasted about how much he loved Jesus and what he would do for Him. Our boasting and conversations should always be how much Jesus loves even someone like me!

The greatest and most amazing supernatural miracle that we receive from God is "Jesus in our hearts," which is Him manifesting His love through us to others to love the unlovable, just like He loves us in all our unloveliness.

"We know that we have passed from death to life, because we love each other. Anyone who does not love remains in death" (1 John 3:14, NIV).

This is not humanly possible.

"This is love: not that we loved God, but that he loved us and sent his Son as an atoning sacrifice for our sins" (1 John 4:10, NIV).

"How great is the love the Father has lavished on us, that we should be called the children of God" (1 John 3:1, NIV).

This love is lavished on every believer, even the ones who I struggle with and the ones who hurt me. If God can send His Son to pay the price for the evil that every man did against Him, how can I tell God that any offense committed against me is too hard for me to forgive through His Spirit? If God asks me to let Him lavish His love on someone through me, how can I say no?

The Lord does not want me to struggle to love people in my own strength but to lay down my own strong feelings, thoughts, attitudes, and beliefs and surrender them to Him (even if they are based on fact). I must choose to let Jesus love that person using my heart, hands, mouth, and mind.

Will I say no to Jesus or will I say yes?

Either way I choose, He will not force His will on me. The Spirit of Jesus wants to manifest His love through His body of believers. The Holy Spirit now speaks through our human voice—the voice of God's children!

Sometimes the relationships we have the hardest time with are the ones that are with the people closest to us. Because of the human love we share, the struggles seem intensified.

This was the lesson the Lord walked me through with someone very close to me: my mom. I carried many traumatic memories and events from my childhood. The Lord has worked so much healing in my heart. He took away the pain of so many of the wounds from my past in such a miraculous, supernatural way.

However, I found myself struggling to show my mom the love she needed. She too carried a lot of wounds and held on to a lot of anger and bitterness from the past.

In 2016, she became terminally ill and went into hospice care. She was able to stay in her apartment the last eight months of her life and not go into a nursing home because my sister and I made the commitment to take turns staying with and taking care of her every day. Every time I went there, it was the same struggle. I would come up short on love because my mom's words or actions caused me to react in an unloving way. When I recognized this pattern, I would literally stop, go to another room, get on my knees, and pray. I would pray for the Spirit to fill my mind and heart with His love for her. The battle I was fighting was to surrender my will, my life, and to let Jesus take over and manifest His love and presence through me.

All the truths about the situation and person are not hidden or overlooked by God; He sees everything about them, and it is in that very moment that He is asking you to let Him love them through you, just where they are.

I did not come to the place where I had victory over my own feelings and attitudes all the time; that would have taken much more time than my mom had! But, praise the Lord, there were many times when I experienced His supernatural love flowing through me. I can tell you that when I surrendered my will and humbled myself before Him on my knees, a peace and a power would come over me that were not of this world (see James 4:10). I would experience such a powerful presence of God that when I would return to my mom, I would have an overwhelming feeling of love and warmth inside my heart. It was like Jesus was right there in the room, and His presence was palpable. The love that would flow from my heart was as strong toward me as it was toward my mom.

You would think that after I experienced this, I would have no trouble from then on with this surrender. Sadly, this was not the case. There are forces of evil that are also at work in these situations, and we must learn to fight and gain freedom over them. It is a real battlefield, and we learn to fight and gain victory little by little. It is a process that takes time and practice. This was a short boot-camp experience, and I learned so much and saw the Lord work in such real and personal ways in my life. It also gave me a real hunger to walk in more of this victory and freedom. I still have a long way to go.

My mom passed away in November 2016. I do not feel guilt or sadness that I did not have the relationship with her that others have with their mom. I know that we both tried to love each other in the strength that we had. What I do have sadness and remorse for is that I refused the Lord many times. When Jesus would ask me, "Can I love your mom through you—unconditionally, unmerited, and undeserved?" Sometimes I chose self-preservation and withheld His love. When I did say yes, it was not that my attitudes and thoughts just disappeared, but they had to give up their "place" when I surrendered them and let the Holy Spirit take first place. They came under His power and authority as I chose Him over self. Being given a glimpse into the victory over self and letting Jesus love through me instead of my own strength, I got to see and experience the powerful love of Jesus. The journey was one of the hardest that the Lord has taken me through so far, but it was one of the most valuable. I am grateful that the Lord loved me enough to walk with me through this valley and allow me to experience His supernatural presence so many times when I yielded to His Spirit. He has changed me in ways that I am amazed and humbled at the same time.

At first glance, when I read the account of the attack against Peter, I thought it was so wrong that God would allow the devil to come after Peter and try to totally destroy him when Jesus had clearly chosen him to be one of His disciples. It seems more logical that God would keep Satan from attacking him.

As referenced earlier in Luke 22:31-32, the Lord actually granted Satan's request to sift Peter like wheat. He let Peter go through this devastating experience because He knew that before Peter could bring the love of Jesus "to feed His sheep," Peter would have to see the true condition of his own heart: the total depravity and lack of love that were there. God in His love allowed this revelation so that Peter would never be deceived again into thinking he could love like Jesus. All he had to offer God now was his weak and broken heart. On the day of Pentecost, Peter was humbly waiting on God for the love he now knew he needed. The Holy Spirit came, and his heart was filled with Jesus' love. He did not start his ministry or calling until he was given this supernatural love and power. Then and only then did Peter have the love that the world needed.

It is Jesus' love that every human heart longs for. Jesus' love has the power to transform someone on the inside, make them whole, and change their lives forever. Only Jesus' love can minister healing to every wound and scar, raise us up out of ashes, and give us new life. Without His love, none of these things are possible. Our human love can never work these miracles.

When I read 1 Corinthians 13, the great love chapter, I understand this to be the description of Jesus' love. The Lord knows that it is not possible for any human to love like this. We cannot even begin to love like this, even to the people closest to us.

These verses have been quoted numerous times. They are spoken at weddings and in sermons, leading people to think that this is an admonishment from the Lord, something He expects us to be able to achieve. This is not the truth. I used to believe this lie that God expects me to love like these verses describe. You do not need to read very far down through this description before, like me, you will be in complete despair and hopelessness at this challenge to love. If you have been struggling with trying to love like Jesus and are feeling hopeless, even angry and frustrated with God, thinking that He is asking you to do something that is impossible, then I have good news. It is impossible! That is why God has not commanded you to love with your weak human heart but to let the supernatural love of Jesus flow through you. Make no mistake, this is one of the greatest challenges as a believer for sure. Being willing to lay down your own life to let His life flow through you requires a daily surrender, but His power is the source to do this too. It will be a process and a journey, but it will be so worth it. Even if the other person does not change, through the process God will transform you to be conformed more to the image of His Son and reflect His glory and light. He will be glorified through your life in ways you never could have imagined. You do not have to live in guilt, condemnation, and defeat any longer, but "you will know the truth, and the truth will set you free" (John 8:32, NIV). You can finally rest in the Lord and let Him do the loving through you.

There is a little more to this story that I would like to share with you, so in the next chapter I will talk about how the Lord used my mom to teach me more about myself and show me even more about God's great love.

I want you to understand that whenever the Lord reveals these hard truths to us about our heart condition and exposes the need for transformation, His motive and desire are always to take us into a deeper level of relationship and freedom in Him.

Chapter 7

MY LESSON IN LOVE

As noted in the previous chapter, one of the biggest love lessons that the Lord walked me through was with my mom. In this chapter, I want to share another part of what I learned. My sincere hope with sharing my testimony is to help you navigate and understand what the Lord might be working in your situation, perhaps hidden to you now.

My mom did not become a believer until she was in her late 50s. We all know what a long process sanctification and maturing in the Lord can be. We are all instantly forgiven and born again, and Jesus issues a full pardon to us. But we have so much to learn, and we grow in our walk with Him ever so slowly. Praise God, He is not in a hurry at all. He will spend a lifetime loving, nurturing, and teaching us the lessons that will ultimately bring us into all the plans and blessings that He wants us to walk in. My mom had her struggles and battles just like we all have as believers. She had some unresolved issues from the fifty years before she became a Christian that she did not address or deal with.

In the later years of her life, she struggled with bitterness and anger at God; she suffered with serious illness and grief over the loss of my father. She was inconsolable. She found herself questioning God about everything. I tried so hard to be a good daughter, to listen to her and encourage her. A lot of my effort was in my own strength and not relying on the Holy Spirit or letting Him do the ministering. Because I was mostly relying on my own limited love and power in the relationship with her, I grew very weary and frustrated. I found myself having a lot of questions as to why these struggles were really necessary.

I myself started questioning God. Just to recap, the circumstances and situation I found myself walking through in 2016 was that my mom was diagnosed with cancer and was put in hospice care. The doctors said she only had weeks to live. Little did anyone know that this hard journey would take eight months to travel through. My heart goes out to anyone who has to walk this path with someone who is dying.

I shared in the previous chapter how God gave me a glimpse into real victory over self and walking in the Spirit. There were many days during this time of training when I experienced what it is like to walk in heavenly realms. When I yielded my will and let Him work and move in me, it was amazing, and His presence was so strong and real. I thank God for His persistent love as He did not give up on me but patiently kept teaching and walking through it with me. I am eternally grateful to Him for all that I learned. The Lord poured out His unconditional love to me during this time, even when sometimes my attitude was proud, self-righteous, and critical about the situation.

This may shock some, but I want to be transparent about my struggles in the hope that it will minister to what you are going through right now. When my mom died, I spent time thinking about what she would be experiencing in heaven. I have to admit that I was still struggling with anger toward her. Now she could see how wrong she had been acting and how hurtful she had been and how stubbornly she had held on to her bitterness and resentment over the things that had been happening to her. I found myself thinking that she would surely have regrets now about being bitter, stubborn, and resentful. I was so disappointed that she never had victory over those things.

It was during this time that the Lord came to me, because of His great love for me, and held the mirror up to me. When I looked into it, I was undone. Now it was my own reflection that I saw. I was judging my mom for the exact same sins that I was looking at in myself. I was stubbornly holding on to my own resentment and anger over the situation.

"Why do you look at the speck of sawdust in your brother's eye and pay no attention to the plank in your own eye?" (Matthew 7:3, NIV).

My sins were laid bare before the Lord. I saw my own attitude, behavior, and the anger I carried. There were so many times I asked the Lord "why" in my own situations. I began to see how much I criticized and complained about what I was going through over those eight months.

The Lord taught me a life-changing lesson through this journey that He took me through with my mom. This new part of the lesson was not about battling and overcoming someone else's behavior but about the Lord finally exposing the wrong attitudes and behavior that were in my own heart. It was not about Him changing someone else but for me to finally find freedom and healing from the hold that resentment and bitterness had on my own heart. The Lord had to expose all the sins in my heart, but only so that He could take the blood of Jesus and wash them away. Then He could apply the healing anointing oil to all the broken places. I wanted my mom to see the truth and get it while she was still alive. God wanted me to see the truth and get it while she was still alive. I feel sadness and regret that I failed to get it while she was here. But because of God's great mercy and His unconditional love for me, He did not give up on me, and I get it now! This is to His glory alone!

I have shared this story in the hope that it will be an encouragement. You may be going through a real struggle with an elderly parent, a spouse, a child, or another loved one. You may be thinking that you should be able to love them and somehow you are failing.

Our enemy always has plenty of accusations to whisper; he loves to drag up the past and open old wounds. The devil's plan is to keep us from walking in the freedom and peace that are ours through Christ. The Lord does not want you to feel guilt and judge yourself for all the weakness and human frailty that you see within yourself, staying stuck there. The Lord knows that unless these wounds and weaknesses are exposed, He cannot heal them and bring you into the freedom and victory He has planned for you.

The Lord's desire is to expose and remove the wrong thinking and behavior that are hindering you from walking in His power and that are weakening your relationship with Him. If you will surrender and lay them all at His feet, the Lord will begin the process of healing your broken heart. He will bring the victory that has always been just out of reach because you had been striving in your own strength. The Lord is waiting to fill you with new hope and courage to work this miracle in your life.

"He heals the brokenhearted and binds up all their wounds" (Psalm 147:3, NIV).

The Lord did heal my broken heart and make it clean and new. When I allowed Him to touch my heart, His Spirit's anointing oil poured out over all the wounds and brought wholeness in a way I had never experienced before.

The Bible tells us that He will "bestow on them a crown of beauty instead of ashes, the oil of joy instead of mourning, and a garment of praise instead of a spirit of despair. They will be called oaks of righteousness, a planting of the Lord for the display of His splendor" (Isaiah 61:3, NIV).

This scripture was written thousands of years ago, but it is the work that the Lord has done in my life today and has the same power to work in your life. It will bring Him the same glory and praise when others see what He has done for you.

Chapter 8

QUESTIONING GOD AFTER DEFEAT

In the book of Joshua, we read the accounts of how the Israelites arrived at the Jordan River after forty years of wandering in the desert. Chapter 1 starts out right after the death of Moses as the people of Israel prepared to cross the Jordan River. The Lord spoke to Joshua and said, "No one will be able to stand up against you all the days of your life. As I was with Moses, so I will be with you; I will never leave you nor forsake you. Be strong and courageous because you will lead these people to inherit the land I swore to their forefathers to give them. Be strong and very courageous. Be careful to obey all the law my servant Moses gave you; do not turn from it to the right or the left, that you may be successful wherever you go" (Joshua 1:5-7, NIV).

These are key scriptures to keep in mind as the events unfold for the Israelites in the promised land. All through Scripture the Lord says that if you are obedient and follow His commands, you will have victory over all your enemies. We play an active part in the battle, but we also must keep our eyes on Jesus. We must let Him be the "Captain of the army" and follow Him in obedience and humility. God parted the Jordan River for Joshua, just like He parted the Red Sea for Moses.

After the spectacular miraculous victory over Jericho, the next city that the Israelites had to face and go up against was the city of Ai. Joshua thought that this little city would be no problem. The Lord had promised him, "No one will be able to stand against you all the days of your life" (Joshua 1:5, NIV).

The Israelite spies went to the city of Ai and told Joshua that he needed to send only two or three thousand men to take the city. Joshua sent about three thousand men, but the Bible does not say that they prayed and asked God if He would give them the victory in this battle. I wonder, if Joshua had sought the Lord before this battle with Ai, would God have revealed to Joshua the hidden sin of Achan?

"So about three thousand went up; but they were routed by the men of Ai, who killed about thirty-six of them. They chased the Israelites from the city gate as far as the stone quarries and struck them down on the slopes. At this the hearts of the Israelites melted and became like water" (Joshua 7:4-5, NIV).

In Joshua 7:6, after this defeat, the Bible says, "Then Joshua tore his clothes and fell face down to the ground before the ark of the Lord . . . The elders of Israel did the same."

Unaware of Achan's sin of stealing some of Jericho's plunder, Joshua became confused and afraid, and he questioned the Lord's motives and His character. Joshua starts his conversation with God by asking,

> Alas, Sovereign Lord, why did you ever bring these people across the Jordan to deliver us into the hands of the Amorites to destroy us? If only we had been content to stay on the other side of the Jordan! Pardon your servant, Lord. What can I say, now that Israel has been routed by its enemies? The Canaanites and the other people of the country will hear about this and they will surround us and wipe out our name from the earth. What then will you do for your own great name? (Joshua 7:7-9, NIV)

This defeat at the hand of the enemy made no sense at all. Joshua tried to use his human thinking and knowledge to figure out what happened, but it failed to show him the truth. His basic sentiment was, if only they had been content to stay where it was safe. After defeat, he was regretting that he was so bold, and he doubted everything.

After parting the waters and taking the Israelites across the Jordan on dry land and into the promised land, as well as the victory at Jericho, Joshua found himself in a place of fear and discouragement. Now, he was even questioning God's calling and anointing on his life. Joshua had become overwhelmed and his faith was shaken because there was no explanation for these new circumstances. It went against everything God had promised him.

But when the Lord answered Joshua, He said, "Stand up! What are you doing down on your face?" (Joshua 7:10, NIV). I think God was saying, "You are wrong about everything that has happened here."

Then the Lord said to him, "Israel has sinned; they have violated my covenant, which I commanded them to keep . . . That is why the Israelites cannot stand against their enemies; they turn their backs and run because they have been made liable to destruction. I will not be with you anymore unless you destroy whatever among you is devoted to destruction" (Joshua 7:11-12, NIV).

After God revealed that it was Achan who had sinned, Joshua confronted him and then Israel stoned him because the Lord had told Joshua that he could not stand against his enemies because of Achan's sin (see Joshua 7:13-26). Then the Lord gave Joshua and the Israelites great victory over the king of Ai and the city. They completely destroyed and burned it, just like Jericho (see Joshua 8).

Sin in the "camp" is behind most battles that are lost to the enemy. Sometimes it is the sins of others that cause defeat and sometimes it is our own. I have discovered that it is not the size of my hidden sin or whatever I am holding on to in my heart but the fact that I am hiding and withholding them from God.

Jesus rescued me out of the kingdom of darkness in 1976 and gave me a new life in Him. I had one victory after another. I was gaining ground back that the enemy had stolen from me. My faith was growing, and the Lord was delivering me from depression, shame, and other strongholds, as well as healing wounds from traumatic events in my life. I experienced God's joy, peace, and promises for the first time.

I was the first person in my family to come to know the Lord and be saved. I thought that the Lord was going to change everyone and remove everything that I struggled with right away. Because of the victories over my past enemies, I was sure that all my present struggles would just be taken care of. However, this did not happen, and I found myself on a long journey through a very dark valley with no end in sight.

During these years, I was able to cover and appear to be walking like a "good Christian soldier," but on the inside, in my heart, I had buried all the pain and hurt. These became my "spoils" from all the battles fought. They were my rightful possessions.

For many years, they remained very well hidden, and I was not even aware of them. But then I started to experience attacks from the enemy where I was not able to gain the victory. I started experiencing depression again, and I did not have the peace and joy anymore that I once enjoyed. I was sure that it was the fault of all the people and circumstances that were in my life at that time. I thought that I had the right to keep these secret thoughts and attitudes hidden in my heart, but these were actually my hidden sins. I thought that they were just feelings and emotions that were a result of what others did to me, not really sin. This was a lie! There is no place for these poisons in the heart of one of God's children. They are from Satan's camp, and we have taken some of his property. They do not belong in the tent of a believer.

Soon I found myself withdrawing from other believers and not telling people about Jesus anymore. I became discouraged, and I neglected praying. I had prayed for God to change the situation, and nothing was changing. I felt a distance and emptiness where there was once such joy and peace. I was convinced that it was the situations and the people in my life that were the root cause of all the difficulty that I was having and all the changes in me.

I was still blind as to why I was walking in defeat. At this time, I decided to take back control of my life. I made some drastic decisions and ended up walking away from the Lord. I laid down my spiritual armor and ran from the battle. My Christian witness suffered much damage, and I caused others to be wounded and hurt. There were innocent casualties among my family and my friends, years wasted. Nothing good came out of my own attempts to fix things, change my circumstances, and get rid of everything I thought was the problem. I still had the hidden things in my heart.

I was suffering constant attacks in my mind from the enemy and living in defeat every day. I lived with tormenting thoughts and whispers in my head that were destructive, accusing, and condemning. The devil told me:

"Nothing will ever change."

"You don't deserve to have anything better."

"Everything is hopeless."

"You have made an unfixable mess of your life."

The enemy would also whisper lies that God did not really love me and that He would not forgive me. After becoming a

Christian, I was now living just like I never knew Him. The devil even quoted scripture to me, saying,

> It is impossible for those who have once been enlightened, who have tasted the heavenly gift, who have shared in the Holy Spirit, who have tasted the goodness of the word of God and the powers of the coming age, and who have fallen away, to be brought back to repentance. To their loss they are crucifying the Son of God all over again and subjecting Him to public disgrace. (Hebrews 6:4-6, NIV)

He would whisper this verse in my head all the time. I was in complete despair and hopelessness. This should not surprise us. He has been whispering lies from the beginning, and he used scripture against Jesus in his attack in the wilderness. Because of my hidden sins, the enemy was able to attack, and I could not get victory over him. I lived with the constant bombardment of lies and negative attitudes and thoughts ruminating in my mind. This was my battlefield.

It took me years to realize that the root problem was these "hidden things" in my heart. Finally, the Lord allowed a life-or-death situation to bring me to the end of myself. It was then that the Lord revealed to me the connection between these hidden sins and the attacks in my mind causing the defeat that I was living in. In His unrelenting grace and undeserved mercy, He stepped right into the darkness with me and delivered me out of it. I was set free from the prison in my mind.

Here's what I want you to understand: the people in my life whom I was struggling with did not change. The Lord did this amazing miracle without changing any of my circumstances or any of the people in my life. Instead, He changed me from the inside out, independent of circumstances.

"So if the Son sets you free, you will be free indeed" (John 8:36, NIV).

In our Old Testament illustration, Achan was not given the chance to repent and be forgiven. Nobody offered to die in his place; he did not get a second chance to have victory over the enemy. What a different story in the New Testament! Jesus came and took our place, canceling the sentence of death that we deserve. He paid the price in full for all our sins, and He died in our place. He can redeem your life if you repent and confess and turn it all over to Him.

"Though your sins are like scarlet, they shall be as white as snow" (Isaiah 1:18, NIV).

He will give you back the ground the enemy has taken, and you can begin to experience victory and blessing again. In my life now, all the endless whispers and chatter from the enemy are gone. This miraculous deliverance occurred about ten years ago, and I am still walking in peace, joy, and victory in Jesus. Satan lost the legal right to all this ground he was holding on to in my life.

If you are struggling like I did and think that you will never be free again or that you have fallen too far, that is a lie from the pit of hell. The Lord is waiting for you to open your heart to Him, unbury all the secret things that are there, and give them to Him. These are the very things that give Satan squatting rights in your heart and life. He knows that as long as you keep them buried and hidden, you will never have victory. The Lord said in Ezekiel 34:27-28, "They will know that I am the Lord, when I break the bars of their yoke and rescue them from the hands of those who enslave them. . . . They will live in safety, and no one will make them afraid" (NIV).

This is a promise of what the Lord is waiting to do for you: "The Lord upholds all who fall and lifts up all who are bowed down" (Psalm 145:14, NIV).

Romans 11:11 talks about the Jews, some of whom were responsible for crucifying Jesus. This living Word of God applies to us today: "Again I ask: Did they stumble so as to fall beyond recovery? Not at all!" (NIV).

Be strong and courageous and entrust yourself into the Father's loving hands. His desire and purpose are to heal and deliver you, to give you peace, joy, and newness of life. You don't have to live in defeat. The Savior died in our place, for the hidden sins in every heart. He is waiting for you to humbly turn back to Him so He can remove the hidden things and restore you to right standing and full relationship with the Lord again.

"Search me, God, and know my heart; test me and know my anxious thoughts. See if there is any offensive way in me, and lead me in the way everlasting" (Psalm 139:23-24, NIV).

The most powerful prayers are the Word of God.

"For the word of God is alive and active. Sharper than any double-edged sword, it penetrates even to dividing soul and spirit, joints and marrow; it judges the thoughts and attitudes of the heart" (Hebrews 4:12, NIV).

The Lord will use the sword of His Spirit to remove all the hidden sins that cause us to live in defeat. This sword may look like a terrifying and deadly weapon that will only cause great pain and death, but when it is in the hands of Jesus, it becomes the very instrument that will bring you the greatest good, the supernatural freedom and healing you need.

The Lord will only remove what is hindering and hurting you. He will only cut away the cords that bind you and the chains that hold you down, for you to walk in victory again. Give all the hidden sins in your heart to Jesus, and let Him forgive you and wash all sin away. He will fill your heart with His love and power so you can walk again in victory and freedom and experience even more than you have ever known before.

To God be all the glory for the things He has done for me. As a popular song says, He is our miracle worker, promise keeper, our light in the darkness. He still saves, delivers, and heals today.

Chapter 9

GOD'S BUILDING PROJECT

I do not know how many of you have studied the book of Ezra, but it speaks a lot to me. Ezra talks about rebuilding God's temple ruins in Jerusalem:

> In the first year of Cyrus king of Persia, in order to fulfill the word of the Lord spoken by Jeremiah, the Lord moved the heart of Cyrus king of Persia to make a proclamation throughout his realm and also to put it in writing.
>
> ". . . The Lord, the God of heaven, has given me all the kingdoms of the earth and he has appointed me to build a temple for him at Jerusalem in Judah." (Ezra 1:2, NIV)

These plans were put in writing as a royal decree that could not be evoked or annulled. This is a shadow of the spiritual journey of the New Testament believers. Before we were saved, we were all in a spiritual state of devastation, and our lives looked just like the ruins of the temple in Jerusalem.

At the time of King Cyrus's reign, the cities and towns had been deserted and lay in ruins, and the Jews had been driven out of the land. All their God-given, rightful ownership and possession of Jerusalem and the temple had been stripped from them by their enemies. This was in the natural realm.

Today the situation is the same for God's children. The Lord, the King of kings, has given His children the rights and authority to take back the ground, to rebuild and establish God's kingdom here on Earth in the spiritual realm. Through the finished work of Jesus and His resurrection power, the dry, barren land and ruins in our lives will be cultivated and planted again.

God wants to rebuild all the damaged, broken places in our lives and the lives of our families. He wants to restore and make these places fruitful and prosperous to bring glory to His name. We can learn much about the process, challenges, and battles that we must fight against our enemies through this historic account of the Jews.

King Cyrus said, "Any of his people among you may go up to Jerusalem in Judah and build the temple of the Lord, the God of Israel, the God who is in Jerusalem, and may their God be with them" (Ezra 1:3, NIV). The king did not do the rebuilding himself; he gave the Jews all his authority, resources, and provisions to go and rebuild Jerusalem and the temple for him.

Every time God starts a building project, He will put on the hearts of His children the desire to rebuild and restore something. This was true then and it is still true today. God always has a perfect blueprint. The Lord will move heaven and Earth for the people He chooses to carry out His plans.

You can be sure that the enemy will also devise a diabolical plan to attempt to block or hinder God's plans all along the way. To help us not be ignorant of his devices, the Lord has given us this rich and detailed account of exactly what happened then and what to expect now. The Lord planned for the rebuilding of the temple long before Cyrus became king of Persia. The Lord is the author and finisher of everything. "Then the family heads of Judah and Benjamin, and the priests and Levites—everyone whose heart God had moved—prepared to go up and build the house of the Lord in Jerusalem" (Ezra 1:5, NIV).

God spoke through His prophet Ezekiel that when Christ the Messiah comes, He would build the temple anew:

> This is what the Sovereign Lord says: On that day I cleanse you from all your sins, I will resettle your towns, and the ruins will be rebuilt. They will say, "This land that was laid waste has become like the garden of Eden; the cities that were lying in ruins, desolate and destroyed, are now fortified and inhabited. Then the nations around you that remain will know that I the Lord have rebuilt what was destroyed and have replanted what was desolate. I the Lord have spoken, and I will do it." (Ezekiel 36:33,35-36, NIV)

Jesus told the religious leaders of His day that if the temple was completely destroyed, He could rebuild it in three days. He was referring to His death and resurrection and to the new temple that would be established in the heart of the believers. It would be a spiritual temple, not made with human hands. This was the

Lord's plan for everyone who receives the Lord Jesus Christ into their heart.

Let us go back and look more closely at what took place in Jerusalem in the book of Ezra. It took awhile for the enemies of Judah to get word of the rebuilding project. When they did, they came to the leader of the Jews, Zerubbabel, and the heads of the families of Israel and said, "Let us help you build because, like you, we seek your God and have been sacrificing to him" (Ezra 4:2, NIV).

These were known enemies of God who had only evil intentions. Their plans were to cause trouble, hinder, and prevent them from completing the work.

Today, when men and women of God are inspired and commissioned to start a new ministry or to step out in faith in a new direction, there will always be worldly and ungodly people who will try to influence them. They will come alongside and appear to want to help or take interest in the project, but their motives are evil. There is always the temptation to compromise so that we do not offend others, or we may start questioning, "Did God really say that only we could do the work?"

Zerubbabel did not have any questions or doubts about the Lord's instructions, nor did he fall for the lies of his enemies. He boldly stated, "You have no part with us in building a temple to our God. We alone will build it for the Lord, the God of Israel, as King Cyrus, the king of Persia, commanded us" (Ezra 4:3, NIV).

This was a bold move and there were immediate consequences for his stand. "Then the peoples around them set out to discourage the people of Judah and make them afraid to go on building. They bribed officials to work against them and frustrate their plans during the entire reign of Cyrus the king of Persia and down to the reign of Darius king of Persia" (Ezra 4:4-5, NIV).

The enemy didn't let up on his attacks. He did everything in his power to stop this project. It was all-out war, not with literal weapons and swords, but with words and accusations, verbal attacks and schemes. These are the same weapons that the enemy uses against us today as we work and build up the kingdom of God in obedience to Him. The enemy sticks closely to his tried-and-proven ways of coming against us, ways he has used over the years against God's people. If we pay close attention to the sequence of events recorded in the Bible, we can preempt some of his attacks. We will always have opposition from the enemy every day, make no mistake about that.

Where do you find yourself in this story? Has the Lord put a passion and a calling on your heart to step out? Is He speaking to rebuild and restore something that the enemy has destroyed and left in ruins?

If you are at the stage in the project where the enemy is actively working to frustrate and work against you, this should be encouraging. It shows that he knows God is moving through this project to restore and bring victory. Your enemy is working to frustrate and stop you, hoping you will abandon God's project. These are three of his primary weapons: intimidation, fear, and discouragement. We read in Ezra that for two years the people worked together as one. The altar and the foundation were finished, and there was a great celebration; with praise and thanksgiving they sang to the Lord. They had successfully completed building the foundation, in spite of all their enemies' attempts to defeat them.

"Despite their fear of the peoples around them, they built the altar on its foundation and sacrificed burnt offerings on it to the Lord, both morning and evening sacrifices" (Ezra 3:3, NIV).

Then the enemy stepped up his attacks again and devised a plan to completely stop the building. After King Cyrus died, the new successor to the throne was King Artaxerxes, who knew nothing about the Jews or the history of the temple. In the beginning of his reign, the enemies of Israel seized the opportunity to write a letter full of accusations and lies against the inhabitants of Judah and Jerusalem to the new king. Their plan worked and the king, with his associates, went immediately to the Jews in Jerusalem and compelled them by force to stop building.

Everything suddenly stopped completely. These evil men had been relentless in their plans and schemes to stop the temple project. After working on the temple for over two years, their enemies had succeeded in getting the reigning king of Persia to force the Jews to stop building.

Then for seventeen years the temple sat unfinished. It looked like the enemy had won. The Jews must have been devastated and questioned God as to why He allowed this to happen. Nobody knows why there was a seventeen-year delay. We know—as we discussed in an earlier chapter—that the Lord's plan is always precise, and it will be fulfilled on the exact day, week, month, and year appointed by Him.

Do not be surprised if, right in the middle of your assignment and plans God has called you to carry out for Him, there is a complete roadblock or obstacle that prevents you from moving forward and even shuts everything down completely for a season. This is a common description of the lives of many Christians today. It was what I experienced in my own life.

Eight years ago, I was led to start writing in notebooks the things that God was revealing to me in my prayer time with Him. Three years ago, I began the process of transferring some of the writings from my notebooks onto the computer and organizing them into chapters for a book. He wanted me to share about His "building project" in my life over the past forty years as a believer.

There were so many things that came against me during this time. There were times I would get frustrated and discouraged and could not understand why the Lord would allow so many hindrances and delay. Then there came a period of time when the project stopped completely. Everything came to a total standstill. I worked very hard and with dedication for a few years and was celebrating the progress I was making; then suddenly everything stopped.

At first, I became frustrated and confused, but the Lord showed me that His desire was for me to rest for a season. My new temporary assignment was to trust and wait in expectation. He had planned the delay. The chapters in the book would be His messages and they would be shared at just the right time—His perfect time!

This book that you are now reading contains some of the writings from my notebooks over those years and the testimony of what the Lord has done in my life over the years. The Lord has been faithful, and in His perfect timing this project has been completed. What a journey it has been. I would not have missed a day of it, because every day I learned something new. I thank God that He gave me the time to just rest and trust Him for a season. This was a real bonus lesson along the way: I learned the priceless value and strength that come from being still, entering into His rest, and abiding in Him in a new and deeper way.

Let's continue to look at the rebuilding of the temple in Ezra 5: after seventeen years had passed, and with the encouragement and support of the prophets Haggai and Zechariah, Zerubbabel once again started the work on rebuilding the temple. The neighboring enemies of the Jews were quick to launch another attack. These men from the neighboring cities went to the next successor and new king, King Darius. The enemies sent a report that read as follows:

> To King Darius: Cordial greetings. The king should know that we went to the district of Judah, to the temple of the

great God. The people are building it with large stones and placing the timbers in the walls. The work is being carried on with diligence and is making rapid progress under their direction. (Ezra 5:7-8, NIV)

They used the same lies and tactics as before to get the king to stop the work again, but this time they failed completely.

Zerubbabel, Joshua, and the heads of the families of Israel sent a response to King Darius and said, "We are the servants of the God of heaven and earth, and we are rebuilding the temple that was built many years ago, one that a great king of Israel built and finished" (Ezra 5:11, NIV). They explained that because of their sins against the Lord, the temple was destroyed by their enemies and they were deported. "However, in the first year of Cyrus king of Babylon, King Cyrus issued a decree to rebuild this house of God" (Ezra 5:13, NIV).

King Darius listened to the leaders of the Jews and Zerubbabel. Then he searched the archives and found the scroll with the decree from King Cyrus concerning the rebuilding of the temple. He immediately sent word and commanded their enemies, saying, "Do not interfere with the work on this temple of God" (Ezra 6:7, NIV).

The king further stated that the expenses for the building project would be fully paid for out of the royal treasury. He issued a decree that if anyone changed this edict, they would be killed. This took place in the second year of King Darius's reign, and so they resumed the rebuilding in the sixth year of his reign.

It was the exact day, week, month, and year that God had planned. Through God's power they experienced great triumph over their enemies before the whole nation, and they celebrated with praise and thanksgiving for the victory He had given them.

This was a foreshadowing of what God had planned to do for us. His building plans in the New Testament were to create a place for His glory to dwell inside the heart of believers. He would create a new heart and come and restore us to be the very temple of the living God, with His Spirit alive in us, filled with His glory and light.

The story that we are learning about in Ezra was the account of the rebuilding of Solomon's temple, originally built many years before and then completely destroyed. This new temple that they built was much smaller and did not begin to compare with the temple Solomon built for God. These Jews had no idea of the magnitude of what they had accomplished for the Lord. All they knew was that they had completed a building project so that they could worship and glorify the Lord. There would be a place for God's Spirit to dwell in their day.

As they looked over the completed structure, they thought the project was finished. They could not ever imagine the glorious plans God had for this new temple. However, the prophet Haggai knew and prophesied at that time that this second temple would one day have a magnificence that would outshine the glory of the first one.

His words were fulfilled after a God-ordained delay of around 500 years, when Joseph and Mary took their boy Jesus to this very temple in Jerusalem. At the temple they met the prophet Simeon. God had promised that he would live to see the Messiah.

> Moved by the Spirit, he went into the temple courts. When the parents brought in the child Jesus to do for him what the custom of the Law required, Simeon took him in his arms and praised God, saying: "Sovereign Lord, as you have promised, you may now dismiss your servant in peace. For my eyes have seen your salvation, which you have prepared in the sight of all nations: a light for revelation to the Gentiles, and the glory of your people Israel." (Luke 2:27-32, NIV)

This temple was filled with the glory of the Lord in a way that could never have been imagined. When the Messiah, the Son of God, walked through those doors, the temple was not just filled with the Spirit of God but with the literal person and presence of the living Christ. God rebuilt the ruins of the temple so that almost 500 years later, Christ the Messiah could enter it and fill it with His glory. This is the same purpose and plan for our lives. God rebuilds and restores the ruins of our lives so that He can come and dwell in us.

What an amazing scene, as the crowds heard the audible voice of Christ, listened to Him teach, and saw Him minister, deliver, and heal. If only the Jews who had rebuilt this temple some 500 years earlier could have been given a glimpse of the

Messiah coming with glory into this place. They were unaware of the honor and privilege they were given to prepare the temple for their Messiah.

We too may be unaware of how huge the impact of the seemingly little assignment that God has given us will be for the kingdom of God for years to come and in eternity.

We have all been given a specific building assignment in the kingdom of God. It is a part of the project that no one else can do, and we have been handpicked to carry it out. Some of us may think that what we are called to do is small and insignificant. But let me assure you that there is no such thing as a small assignment in God's building project. Every part in the building of God's kingdom is vital and will always have far-reaching effects, eternal worth, and lasting rewards. In the accounts of the struggles of the saints of old, they all worked faithfully and with courage and persistence in what they were called to do. Each one worked on his assignment and they all rejoiced and celebrated together when it was complete because each one had done his part. The Bible says, "For everything that was written in the past was written to teach us, so that through the endurance taught in the Scriptures and the encouragement they provide we might have hope" (Romans 15:4, NIV).

The Lord is the Creator and the architect of everything in heaven and on Earth. He does not ask for our advice or expect us to figure out the best plan. Before time, the Lord had the perfect plan and orchestrated all the details so that His purpose would be accomplished.

What part do we play in God's building projects? What has He called us to do? Where do we get the strength and power to achieve such impossible projects? What are the necessary tools and equipment needed for building projects in the kingdom of God today?

We do not use merely brick, wood, and mortar, but today's projects are also in the spirit realm. They always begin with fervent prayer, seeking to achieve God's spiritual purposes and plans as our priority and His glory as the ultimate outcome. We need the anointing and power of our King of kings to go forth in His authority and sovereign rule and lordship. We must be dressed for the battle that we know lies ahead. Through prayer we must cover everything in the blood of Jesus.

In the New Testament, Paul gives detailed instructions for us to put on the armor of God daily and take our position in the ranks of God's army:

- Put our belt of truth around our waist. Everything must start with the living Word.

- We need to put on the breastplate of righteousness, not standing in any of our own goodness or works but only accepting the covering of the righteousness of Christ.

- Our feet fitted with the readiness that comes from the gospel of peace. Figuratively, God gives us a pair of shoes that fit us perfectly and are designed to enable us to walk the path set before us. These shoes will take us to the people and places to share the good news of reconciliation and peace.

- The shield of faith, with which we can extinguish all the flaming arrows of the evil one, such as the arrows, evil words, and cruel attacks from Satan. If your shield is too heavy for you to hold right now, then get your brothers and sisters in the Lord to hold you up through their faith and prayers.

- The helmet of salvation covers our mind with the blood of Jesus.

- Last, we wield the sword of the Spirit, which is the Word of God. A deadly weapon against our enemies, we pray in the Spirit and speak the Word out loud. We use it against all the swords and arrows of the enemy. We learn to listen to the Spirit and allow Him to empower us and give us instructions for battle strategies every day! (See Ephesians 6.)

Our real enemies are the demonic spirits that are invisible and behind the scenes, calling the shots. Wherever you are finding yourself in the building project that God has given you, do not lose heart. Maybe you are working hard and the attacks from the enemy are wearing you down. Maybe you do not feel like you will be able to stand against it anymore. Or perhaps the project has come to a complete stop, you are discouraged or confused, and your faith has been shaken.

The scriptures say,

The Lord is my light and my salvation—whom shall, I fear? The Lord is the stronghold of my life—of whom shall I be afraid? When the wicked advance against me to devour me, it is my enemies and my foes who will stumble and fall. Though an army besiege me, my heart will not fear; . . . For in the day of trouble he will keep me safe in his dwelling; he will hide me in the shelter of his tent. (Psalm 27:1-3,5, NIV)

I know whom I have believed and am convinced that he is able to guard what I have entrusted to him until that day. (2 Timothy 1:12, NIV)

My flesh and my heart may fail, but God is the strength of my heart and my portion forever. (Psalm 73:26, NIV)

The Lord is the everlasting God, the Creator of the ends of the earth. He will not grow tired or weary, and his understanding no one can fathom. He gives strength to the weary and increases the power of the weak. Even youths grow tired and weary, and young men stumble and fall; but those who hope in the Lord will renew their strength. They will soar on wings like eagles; they will run and not grow weary, they will walk and not be faint. (Isaiah 40:28-31, NIV)

All scripture is alive and God-breathed. Slowly and prayerfully read over these verses and let the Spirit of the living

Christ breathe life into your weary soul. He is the One who is waiting to empower, revive, renew, and restore you again.

My prayer is that the lessons and experiences of these men of the Old Testament will bring encouragement, new hope, and courage as you faithfully work on the assignment the Lord has called you to. Their endurance and perseverance will inspire you. Know they have gone before you as a "great cloud of witness" throughout the ages, and they are cheering you on in heaven. They have experienced the same attacks and struggles, and the Lord has faithfully brought them through to victory, every time. The Lord is the same yesterday, today, and forever. What He has done for them, He will do for you!

Chapter 10

STANDING UP FOR GOD AGAINST GIANTS

In this chapter, I want to bring new insight through the account of the courageous and faithful man Noah.

In Genesis 1:27-28 we read the account of the Lord creating Adam and Eve and blessing them. They enjoyed a perfect relationship and fellowship with God in purity and holiness. How rapidly the scene deteriorated once sin entered into the picture. The Bible account of Noah's life begins in Genesis 5. Noah was thought to be only 9 or 10 generations after Adam and Eve.

"The Lord saw how great the wickedness of the human race had become on the earth, and that every inclination of the thoughts of the human heart was only evil all the time" (Genesis 6:5, NIV).

It is hard for me to even imagine that all the people on Earth were so wicked and evil that none of them ever had a godly, or even moral, motive or thought about anything. This is not talking about just worldly or selfish people. This was a time on Earth when everyone had totally rejected and rebelled against

God and had sold out to every kind of evil their minds could imagine or hearts could conceive. There was also another group of people that are described in this Bible account that were even more evil. In Genesis 6:4 it says, "The Nephilim were a race of giants that existed on the earth at the time of Noah, before the flood."

"When men began to increase in number on the earth and daughters were born to them, the sons of gods saw that the daughters of humans were beautiful, and they married any of them they chose" (Genesis 6:1, NIV).

The Jewish interpreters of the Bible unanimously believe that the "sons of gods" were the Nephilim—giants and notoriously wicked. Their influence on the human race was profoundly evil. Noah was up against giants too.

In the latter portion of Numbers 13, after the Israelites reached the promised land, Moses sent men to explore the land, and after forty days they returned to Moses, giving an account and description of giants occupying the land of Canaan. The spies told Moses, "All the people we saw there are of great size. We saw the Nephilim there (the descendants of Anak come from the Nephilim). We seemed like grasshoppers in our own eyes, and we looked the same to them" (Numbers 13:32-33, NIV).

The people occupying the promised land are described in the Hebrew Bible as a literal race of giants. There were over two million Israelites in Moses' day who were all told to take courage and face these "giants," but they were too afraid. They were filled with fear and unbelief.

Now, in stark contrast, let's look back and consider that Noah stood alone against the giants of his day. He was a believer in God and a righteous man (one who was just and had right standing with God). He is called blameless in his generation. The evil people of Noah's day were violent and hostile, with evil attitudes and corrupt hearts, and some were giants.

We have all been around people who hate God. You can feel the darkness that emanates from them. It takes all the courage and faith we can muster to stand against it. Likewise, this man of God did not run in fear, and he did not back down or let others intimidate him from walking with the Lord in righteousness. Noah walked with God in this evil generation for 500 years. If that was not amazing enough, and seemingly humanly impossible, the Lord shared with him the coming judgment that He would bring and what He wanted Noah to do next.

> God saw how corrupt the earth had become, for all the people on earth had corrupted their ways. So God said to Noah, "I am going to put an end to all people, for the earth is filled with violence because of them. I am surely going to destroy both them and the earth. So make yourself an ark of cypress wood; make rooms in it and coat it with pitch inside and out. Everything on earth will perish. But I will establish my covenant with you, and you will enter the ark—you and your sons and your wife and your sons' wives with you. (Genesis 6:12-14,17-18, NIV)

God was telling Noah to build a boat because He was going to cause it to rain and flood the earth. Noah had never seen rain. Noah did not even know what God was talking about, but this man of God did everything that the Lord commanded.

We can be sure the Lord gave Noah a supernatural faith and strength to face so much evil and walk in such total obedience. It is a real testimony of God's unlimited provision. Whatever He calls us to do, He will equip us with the measure of faith and courage equal to the task.

This assignment also would have called for steady endurance with the mundaneness and drudgery of getting up every morning to face the same tasks and doing the same thing for 100 years, working slowly on this ark and every day making such little progress, maybe not even seeing any noticeable progress for years. This task was far from an exciting adventure. Did Noah ever wonder if this was really the way the Lord wanted him to spend the rest of his life? When would this assignment ever end?

Is this starting to sound familiar to you?

Have you been called to work on a God-ordained project that will likely take you the rest of your life? You have struggled alone and with great opposition, and your progress is so slow that you have to look back years to even recognize any sign of it. Part of God's plan was developing and working with Noah on the inside. He was preparing him for the future assignment after the flood, when he came out of the ark and had to begin again to build and plant and establish a life. I know that one thing Noah would have learned over the 100 years of building the ark was to depend on God alone, probably more than any man who ever lived on Earth.

Remember, Noah would have been 600 years old when he began this next phase of his assignment. After the flood, Noah was given the responsibility of starting from scratch and establishing everything once again. There was more building and planting and work to be done.

None of us knows what our next assignment will be, but I can assure you that everything you are doing now and everything you are experiencing or learning is to prepare for your next assignment. All of it is vitally necessary and ordained by the Lord. Our next assignment may be here on Earth or it may be in heaven. Noah's life story can give us all so much insight and encouragement regarding the struggles and battles that we face today and God's bigger plans for our future.

During the time of the construction of the Ark, everyone around would have been watching Noah's life and this strange project he had undertaken: building a boat in the middle of dry land. God displayed His great mercy to everyone over those years and gave every person the chance to repent and turn to Him, to believe in this God that Noah served. It would be hard to imagine that there was anyone living at that time who did not see or hear about the ark Noah was building and the reason behind it.

These people spent the whole 100-plus years enjoying their evil and wicked lives, while Noah faithfully worked hard every day in what the Lord called him to do. We have not worked under such extreme circumstances for 100 years like this humble man, but Noah was God's anointed witness in his generation. He was a righteous man who walked with God, and God's Spirit was with him for all to see.

The Bible says very little about Noah's family, only that Methuselah was the father of Lamech, Noah's father, and had other sons and daughters. They would have been Noah's aunts and uncles. Then the Bible says, "After Noah was born, Lamech lived 595 years and had other sons and daughters" (Genesis 5:30, NIV)—Noah's brothers and sisters.

Sadly, none of Noah's family that were still living at the time of the flood repented or turned to the Lord. Noah had to enter the ark with his wife, sons, and their wives. Noah's heartache and pain must have been great, and what grief and sorrow he must have experienced. Imagine the courage and strength it would have taken to leave any family member behind and enter the ark on that day. "The Lord then said to Noah, 'Go into the ark, you and your whole family, because I have found you righteous in this generation'" (Genesis 7:1, NIV). "Seven days from now I will send rain on the earth for forty days and forty nights, and I will wipe from the face of the earth every living creature I have made" (v. 4, NIV).

Noah entered the ark seven days before the flood started. The door to the ark remained open those seven days, but no one else ever came through the door. If I had been in Noah's shoes,

I would have been praying hard and hoping that some of my extended family would walk through that door, but not one ever did.

"Then the Lord shut him in" (Genesis 7:16, NIV).

As heartbreaking as it was for Noah to leave behind everything and everyone to be obedient to God and follow Him, I think about how much greater the heartbreak and pain were that the Lord felt at this time. To watch all His creation and all the people die. The Lord is not the author of death but the giver of life.

"The Lord saw how great the wickedness of the human race had become on the earth, and that every inclination of the thoughts of the human heart was only evil all the time. The Lord regretted that he had made human beings on earth, and his heart was filled with pain" (Genesis 6:5-6, NIV).

How tragic that God was totally rejected and hated by all the people on Earth, by everyone that He had created, loved, blessed, and cared for all their lives. To think that our sins can cause the heart of God to be filled with pain is a sobering thought. When I am struggling with a decision or a temptation, I pray that I will remember that my choice will either bring joy to my Father's heart or pain and grief.

Satan's plans and schemes are always about inflicting as much pain and causing the maximum suffering and damage as possible in our lives. We need to realize that this is not the enemy's ultimate objective in all his plans; his real goal is to inflict the maximum amount of pain and suffering to God's heart.

Satan knows he is no match for God. He uses his diabolical schemes to attack the Lord through hurting His sons and daughters created in His image. The devil had successfully deceived and overpowered the people of Noah's time for the specific purpose of wiping out any image of God on this earth. This was his ultimate scheme and plan: to contaminate and corrupt everything that God had created so that God in His holiness would have no choice but to destroy all the evil. Satan thought that he had won and that he had forced the Lord to destroy all His creation on Earth with only one family left. He must have thought that surely this one family would be easy to pick off later, and then the whole job would be done.

The story does not end there. The Lord was in complete control and His plan of redemption and salvation was revealed prophetically through these events. In heaven, the plan was unfolding and would not fail. The Lord would restore and renew all life and bring salvation to everyone.

"I now establish my covenant with you and your descendants after you . . . Never again will all life be destroyed by the waters of a flood; never again to destroy the earth. And God said, 'This is the sign of the covenant I am making between me and you and every living creature with you, a covenant for all generations to come: I have set my rainbow in the clouds, and it will be the sign of the covenant between me and the earth'" (Genesis 9:9,11-13, NIV).

Satan heard God make a covenant with Noah and promise to never again destroy the earth because of mankind's wickedness.

God knew that the sin nature of man and his unredeemed heart were not destroyed in the flood. Evil had not been destroyed, only evil men. There would one day come the Messiah, the Savior who would defeat evil and make a way for every man to be forgiven and rescued from the flood of evil that will destroy their lives. He would rescue us from the coming judgment. God cannot and will not ever break His promises to us. Satan knows that God cannot lie.

In the New Testament, we see another Man, Jesus, who came and preached judgment and repentance to the wicked and lost generation of His day. Jesus came to bring the kingdom of God to Earth and to establish a new covenant with His people. The Lord has made a way for all mankind to escape the coming judgment and to be carried to safety. There will be a day that will come—just as the flood of Noah's day—the last day for men to make the choice to repent and get in the boat and to receive the Savior, Jesus.

The Lord has been patient and merciful for thousands of years while the message of the good news of Jesus is spread all over the earth until everyone has heard it and been given a chance to accept and receive it. The Lord's kindness and grace keep Him from coming back now. The hearts of men today are surely as wicked as the days of Noah. The Bible says, "The Lord is not slow in keeping his promise, as some understand slowness. Instead he is patient with you, not wanting anyone to perish, but everyone to come to repentance" (2 Peter 3:9, NIV).

So we are all called to be the Noah of our day, in our families and the place where the Lord has planted us on Earth. The Lord's coming is near, and we have very little time left to warn and tell the story of Jesus, His love, and His promises to this dying world. Noah did not know exactly when the Lord would bring the flood and when the end would come. If the Lord gave him the strength and grace to stand, to keep going and to not give up, then we can take great comfort knowing that God can give us the same grace and strength to go on, whatever we face. All scripture is given to encourage us so that we can know this God of Noah. If you want to know the Lord in such a real way, you can enter into a relationship with Him where He can show His strength and glory to you and through you. Then you can experience His power, deliverance, mercy, and grace, standing against giants and defeating them.

"Have I not commanded you? Be strong and courageous. Do not be afraid; do not be discouraged, for the Lord your God will be with you wherever you go" (Joshua 1:9, NIV).

There is such encouragement in this account of Noah. He was a man who lived before the days of Jesus and before the Holy Spirit was given to believers. His life was lived by faith alone, and he trusted and believed that everything that the Lord said was truth. Noah considered his relationship with the Lord more important than anything or anyone in his life. I pray that my life would look like that.

This account also gives greater insight into the real battle waged against me. The real purpose and plan are to inflict pain and suffering on my Father, to try to discredit His name, and to destroy everyone and everything that He has so lovingly created that bears His image. All that the devil brings against me is not really because he cares what I do or say. I am only a means to an end.

He has been at war with God long before the earth was formed or any man or woman ever walked on it. The devil's hatred and rage against God are great; he has been pure evil ever since he was thrown out of heaven.

"He replied, 'I saw Satan fall like lightning from heaven. I have given you authority to trample on snakes and scorpions, and over all the power of the enemy; nothing will harm you'" (Luke 10:18-19, NIV).

The battle is a heavenly battle, and it has already been won by the Lord Jesus Christ. Satan is already defeated and has lost his power. The devil needs a human brain to devise his evil schemes, human hands to carry them out, human feet to take him where he wants to go, and a human voice to speak his evil words and curses. He needs a host to inhabit (see Romans 6:13-16).

Our battles are not against the person but against the spirit possessing and controlling that person. The real attack is targeted at the Lord whom we serve. This is such powerful knowledge and helps me so much to understand the way the enemy works and the motives and purpose for his attacks against me. I have a new passion and resolve to fight and defend the Lord's name and honor. It is not about me; it is about my Father.

Noah was called to a difficult and overwhelming assignment for just one man to accomplish, and yet he accomplished everything that God called him to do. We truly serve a God of the impossible. You may be saying that the task in front of you is impossible for you; you may be struggling with doubt and fear that you can never stay the course and finish what the Lord has called you to do. Like the giants of Noah's day, you are also called to face giants. These giants may not be in physical stature but in the spirit realm. They are demonic and far exceed our strength and abilities to fight and win.

You are absolutely right that you cannot do it! Thanks be to Jesus; the Lord has not called you to do anything in your own strength and ability. The Lord always calls us to the assignments that are impossible and beyond our ability. He is always looking for the humble and trusting servant who will respond to His call and say, "Here I am, Lord," in blind obedience and total surrender to Him.

Letting the Lord work through you is the most amazing and supernatural plan that is purposed in His heart. If you have answered the call of God but find yourself alone and weary, battle fatigued and out of strength, without passion to keep going, be encouraged because the Lord already knew that these days would come to you. The Lord made provision in advance and has the supplies and equipment needed for the next phase. He also has all the grace, strength, and passion you need. His living water will quench your deepest thirst, and His living manna will satisfy your deepest hunger.

Whatever the specific hindrance—spiritual, emotional, or physical need—Jesus is more than you need. Maybe this story is the way the Lord will encourage you and fill you with new hope and power. Maybe it will be something else that He brings into your life very soon. I am praying for you and know that the answer and provision are coming soon. Hold on, stay humble, and fix your eyes on Jesus for just a little longer.

If the Lord was able to call and raise Noah up to work such an impossible and God-sized task, then He is more than able to work His plans and purposes out through His sons and daughters today who have His Holy Spirit living and moving inside of them. You have the resurrection power of Jesus Christ Himself working in your life. I speak and declare for you all the scriptures that are written out below. They are alive and powerful. All His promises are faithful and true!

> His divine power has given us everything we need for life and godliness through our knowledge of him who called us by his own glory and goodness. Through these he has given us his very great and precious promises, so that through them you may participate in the divine nature, having escaped the corruption in the world caused by evil desires. (2 Peter 1:3-4, NIV)

> The Son is the radiance of God's glory and the exact representation of his being, sustaining all things by his powerful word. (Hebrews 1:3, NIV)

I pray that out of his glorious riches he may strengthen you with power through his Spirit in your inner being, so that Christ may dwell in your hearts through faith. (Ephesians 3:16-17, NIV)

I pray, "May the God of hope fill you with all joy and peace as you trust in him, so that you may overflow with hope by the power of the Holy Spirit" (Romans 15:13, NIV).

Amen.

Chapter 11

WHERE GOD CHOOSES TO DWELL

As the Creator and God of all things, visible and invisible, the Lord lacks nothing and possesses everything. He has proven through the Word and His Son, Jesus, that His greatest heart's desire is to share His life and all He has created with us.

Did you ever think about all God's dwelling places? I find it so amazing that God chose the nation of Israel to be His very own people. He knew that they could not come to heaven and dwell with Him while they lived in their mortal bodies. The only way He could be with them all the time was to come to Earth. He commissioned Moses to draw up the plans for a tabernacle, which would be a dwelling place for the glory and Spirit of God to dwell among His people. The Lord told Moses, "Then have them make a sanctuary for me, and I will dwell among them. Make this tabernacle and all its furnishings exactly like the pattern I will show you" (Exodus 25:8-9, NIV).

This sanctuary was a tent. This is where the presence of the Lord would dwell.

What would make the Creator and Lord of heaven and Earth ever desire to leave His holy heaven with all its beauty, purity, and perfection, and come to Earth with all its impurity, evil, and wickedness? The answer is love; He chose relationship with man. He knew that humans would continually rebel and would never really love Him the way that He deserves to be loved. Most of the time it would be a pretty one-sided relationship. The Israelites quickly fell into rebellion, murmuring, complaining, and turning their backs on Him. They were so easily persuaded to follow after other gods. These are the children that the Lord brought out of Egypt with a mighty hand; He chose them to be His people and He would be their God. It was all His choice to come, to save, and to deliver. Even more so, God chose to now dwell with them.

The Israelites spent years living in deserts, battling the evil nations around them, and moving around in tents with no permanent place to dwell. And the Lord of the universe chose to live in a tent among them.

Many years later, King David was the first person to notice that he himself was living in a luxurious palace "like a king," while the Lord was still living in a tent. It had not occurred to anyone that maybe the King of kings was worthy of a more respectable dwelling place. David said to Nathan the prophet, "Here I am, living in a house of cedar, while the ark of God remains in a tent" (2 Samuel 7:2, NIV).

David had it in his heart to build a temple fit for the Almighty God's Spirit to dwell in. It would be grander and greater than anything ever built. It would be a place where all the people could come close to the Lord, to pray and worship Him. They would experience redemption and rescue from all their enemies, and restoration and rebuilding for their nation were coming true during this time. Justice was served up to their enemies through David's and Solomon's reigns as kings. All the world would stand in awe of the God of Israel. He allowed the temple to be built because of His extravagant love for them. God knew before it was built that the people would not keep their covenant with Him. They would defile this temple and bring shame and disgrace to God's name, and He would have to completely destroy it one day.

For a season and a time, however, God would use it to reveal Himself to the people in a deeper way, and it would be a glimpse of His throne room and dwelling place in heaven. This temple project began with King David and would be built during the reign of Solomon. It would be an exact replica of the one in heaven.

This speaks volumes about the heart of God. He is like no other god. He lived with His people and stayed close to them as they wandered through the wilderness. How different from the kings and rulers of this world, who live in lofty palaces and demand that everyone provide for their every need as they indulge in every luxury and desire of their heart. They think they are entitled and worthy of all honor and privilege. How much more is the Lord worthy of all honor, glory, praise, and privilege. The Lord did not watch from far away in heaven, but His Spirit was present in the tabernacle here on Earth during the time of Moses, forty years in the wilderness, and until Solomon became king of Israel around 480 years later.

"Now Moses used to take a tent and pitch it outside the camp some distance away, calling it the 'tent of meeting.' Anyone inquiring of the Lord would go to the tent of meeting outside the camp. As Moses went into the tent, the pillar of cloud would come down and stay at the entrance, while the Lord spoke with Moses. The Lord would speak to Moses face to face as one speaks to a friend" (Exodus 33:7,9,11, NIV).

The Lord never asked or demanded a temple. He told King David, "I have not dwelt in a house from the day I brought the Israelites up out of Egypt to this day. I have been moving from place to place with a tent as my dwelling. Wherever I have moved with all the Israelites, did I ever say to any of their rulers whom I commanded to shepherd my people, 'Why have you not built me a house of cedar?'" (2 Samuel 7:6-7, NIV).

True to His loving character, His thoughts were for His people. He is the Good Shepherd, and He dwells with His flock. "But he brought his people out like a flock; he led them like sheep through the desert" (Psalm 78:52, NIV)

Jesus, when He came to Earth to live, showed even more clearly what the heart of the Father was like. God was willing to send His Son to Earth to dwell in a human body (a tent) and walk with His people and minister to them hands-on, sharing all their human struggles with them in person.

If that was not amazing enough, He chose to be abused, beaten, and crucified for us. This is amazing love! This was the Lord Almighty, the King of kings, and Creator of all things. When Jesus was crucified, the veil in the temple was torn in two. Jesus established a new and living way into the Holy of Holies where the Lord dwelt.

"For Christ did not enter a man-made sanctuary that was only a copy of the true one, He entered heaven itself, now to appear for us in God's presence. Therefore, brothers, since we have confidence to enter the Most Holy Place by the blood of Jesus, by a new and living way opened for us through the curtain, that is His body, and since we have a high priest over the house of God, let us draw near to God with a sincere heart in full assurance of faith" (Hebrews 9:24,19-22, NIV).

God moved out of this man-made temple in Jerusalem when Christ was crucified, and He would never dwell there again. In the New Testament Paul states that God no longer dwells in the temple in Jerusalem: "The God who made the world and everything in it is the Lord of heaven and earth and does not live in temples built by hands" (Acts 17:24, NIV).

"This temple would be made desolate, destroyed forever just as Jesus prophesied to Jerusalem: 'Look, your house is left to you desolate, I tell you, you will not see Me again until you say, Blessed is He who comes in the name of the Lord'" (Luke 13:35, NIV).

The temple was destroyed by the Romans in AD 70 just as Jesus prophesied.

He did not move into the temple as the reigning king; instead He became a humble servant to the people who came to hear Him preach. The temple was built for Jesus as much as the Father and the Spirit—a place for all the Godhead to dwell. However, Jesus did not dwell in this man-made temple in Jerusalem. He remained homeless and traveled to the towns and cities where He ministered to the people there.

After the resurrection and ascension of Christ, we see the third person of the Trinity, the Holy Spirit, come to take up residence and dwell in God's people (see 1 Corinthians 6:19).

Jesus said, "But I tell you the truth: It is for your good that I am going away. Unless I go away, the Counselor will not come to you, but if I go, I will send Him to you. When He comes, He will convict the world of guilt in regard to sin and righteousness and judgment" (John 16:7-8, NIV).

"But when he, the Spirit of truth, comes, he will guide you into all truth" (John 16:13, NIV).

"You, dear children, are from God and have overcome them, because the one who is in you is greater than the one who is in the world" (1 John 4:4, NIV).

Satan is no match for the Holy Spirit. He stands guilty and condemned of murdering the innocent Son of God. Jesus now reigns over all of heaven and Earth. Just like Jesus spoke only what the Father told Him, now the Holy Spirit will speak only what He hears from Jesus. He will testify about Jesus: the message of the gospel is alive and quickened by the Holy Spirit.

"But you will receive power when the Holy Spirit comes on you; and you will be my witnesses in Jerusalem, and in all Judea and Samaria, and to the ends of the earth" (Acts 1:8, NIV).

"Suddenly a sound like the blowing of a violent wind came from heaven and filled the whole house where they were sitting. They saw what seemed to be tongues of fire that separated and came to rest on each of them. All of them were filled with the Holy Spirit and began to speak in other tongues as the Spirit enabled them" (Acts 2:2-4, NIV).

In the Old Testament, God the Father lived in a tent, and then in the New Testament, His Son came to Earth as the Son of man and lived without any home at all. Then if that were not amazing enough, God humbled Himself even further and has chosen to dwell, through His Spirit, in the hearts of those who believe in Jesus. This great and glorious King of kings, the all-powerful and mighty God has taken up residence in our hearts. This ultimate expression of God's passionate desire is to always be with us through everything, every day of our lives; He chose to dwell in our hearts.

Paul followed Christ's example and said, "Your attitude should be the same as that of Christ Jesus, who being in very nature God, did not consider equality with God something to be grasped, but made Himself nothing, taking the very nature of a servant, being made in human likeness. And being found in the appearance as a man, He humbled Himself and became obedient to death, even death on a cross" (Philippians 2:5-8, NIV).

Jesus never owned His own home. He owned no possessions here on Earth. He was a carpenter by trade, but there are no accounts of Him purchasing or storing up any money or personal property or possessions. He was totally focused on the needs of others and took no thought for Himself or any of His own wants or needs.

Jesus warns, "Then he said to them, 'Watch out! Be on your guard against all kinds of greed; life does not consist in an abundance of possessions'" (Luke 12:15, NIV).

"Then he [the rich man] said, 'This is what I will do. I will tear down my barns and build bigger ones and there I will store my surplus grain. And I'll say to myself, "You have plenty of grain laid up for many years. Take life easy; eat, drink and be merry'" (Luke 12:18, NIV).

This man was worried about building a big barn for his stuff. This is the heart and mind of the world, and Satan, and is the complete opposite of our loving heavenly Father. Even though it was the Lord who had blessed him with everything he had, this man's heart was only filled with himself and earthly things like the barns. He was dwelling in a palace with no regard or desire to make room for the Lord and a place for Him to dwell in his life and heart. This rich man perished without the Lord.

If the Holy Spirit dwells in us, our lives will reflect the heart of God and we will be devoted to Him. We will be encouraged to give out of a grateful heart, knowing that anything that we possess is only because God provided us with it. As we store up treasures in heaven, our concern is more about being a "temple" filled with His Spirit for all the world to see, displaying His beauty and presence and drawing people to Him.

"In him the whole building is joined together and rises to become a holy temple in the Lord. And in him you too are being built together to become a dwelling in which God lives by his Spirit" (Ephesians 2:21-22, NIV).

God has promised us that nothing would ever separate us from His love forever. "Who shall separate us from the love of Christ? Shall trouble or hardship, persecution or famine or nakedness or danger or sword?" (Romans 8:35, NIV).

"No, in all these things we are more than conquerors through him who loved us. For I am convinced that neither death nor life, neither angels nor demons, neither the present nor the future, nor any powers, neither height nor depth, nor anything else in all creation, will be able to separate us from the love of God that is in Christ Jesus our Lord" (Romans 8:37-39, NIV).

My heart is full of gratitude and praise, and I stand in awe of the Lord. There is nothing in my life now or anything in the future that I would ever have to go through without the Lord being with me. Nothing in the natural world and nothing in the spiritual world can separate me from the Lord. We have a strong and secure fortress and place of safety because the Lord dwells in us. He has made sure that we can never be apart from Him, and He has promised to never leave or forsake us. What courage and confidence we can find in these faithful promises.

All of Scripture is the story of God's love for us. He has never changed His mind, and He never will, even when His children turn away and reject Him. From the creation of Adam, the Lord has never given up on His children. God has suffered pain and heartbreak countless times as His children constantly wander away and turn to all kinds of other worldly loves, people, and things that steal their hearts away from Him. All along His plans and His heart's desire were to make His home, His permanent dwelling place, in our heart. He made this promise: "The Lord himself goes before you and will be with you; he will never leave you or forsake you. Do not be afraid; do not be discouraged" (Deuteronomy 31:8, NIV).

Paul's testimony was, "I believe everything that is in accordance with the Law and that is written in the Prophets, and I have the same hope in God as these men themselves have, that there will be a resurrection of both the righteous and the wicked" (Acts 24:14-15, NIV).

Many of the saints of the Old Testament were living by faith until the day they died but never received the things that God promised them. "All these people were still living by faith when they died. They did not receive the things promised; they only saw them and welcomed them from a distance, admitting that they were foreigners and strangers on earth" (Hebrews 11:13, NIV).

God comes to dwell in us because He loves us; however, that doesn't mean that every problem is fixed here on Earth.

The gospel reveals that even if you have to wait for some answers, the Holy Spirit will give you the power and grace you need to walk in hope and assurance that you have an inheritance kept for you, a permanent dwelling place with Him.

No matter what happens in this life, when we make a decision to repent of our sins and believe in Jesus, there is the promise of eternal relationship and life with Him. This is what we rejoice in and praise the Lord for. There is coming a day when God's righteous judgment will be revealed.

"To those who by persistence in doing good seek glory, honor and immortality, he will give everyone eternal life. But for those who are self-seeking and who reject the truth and follow evil, there will be wrath and anger" (Romans 2:7-8, NIV).

"Praise be to the God and Father of our Lord Jesus Christ! In his great mercy he has given us new birth into a living hope through the resurrection of Jesus Christ from the dead, and into an inheritance that can never perish, spoil or fade. This inheritance is kept in heaven for you, who through faith are shielded by God's power until the coming of the salvation that is ready to be revealed in the last time. In all this you greatly rejoice, though now for a little while you may have had to suffer grief in all kinds of trials" (1 Peter 1:3-6, NIV).

Let us never lose sight of what our hope is anchored on and that the Lord dwelling in us forever is a profound act of love. Praise the Lord for His endless love and all that He has done for us so that we could know Him and experience a real relationship with Him, and that Jesus will share His full inheritance with us someday in heaven. The Lord has made a way for us to dwell with Him forever because of His eternal plan and passionate desire to share His life with us.

Chapter 12

STORY OF DANIEL

Daniel is another man of God in the Bible who was full of faith, and he gives me such hope and encouragement to live for God in the midst of an evil generation. He had so much character and perseverance, and we can learn much from his example. We have all experienced trials, such as facing injustice, deliberate evil, and wrongdoing from people. Why wouldn't our loving Father just come down and fix it, defeating our enemies right away when we pray to Him?

Is it really God's plan to keep us safe and secure from all trials and evil?

Why doesn't He just prosper us, bless us, and give us only good things in life?

I have gone through trials that have lasted for years, and there are some battles that I am still fighting today. This is part of my testimony to God's great power and love displayed in and through my life. People all around me are closely watching me, hoping to see if the God I serve is real. They want evidence that

God does deliver and still works miracles today because they so desperately need a miracle in their own life.

This was true in Daniel's day as well. People were watching to see if the God he served was real.

This is how Jerusalem was taken:

> In the ninth year of Zedekiah king of Judah, in the tenth month, Nebuchadnezzar king of Babylon marched against Jerusalem with his whole army and laid siege to it. The Babylonians set fire to the royal palace and the houses of the people and broke down the walls of Jerusalem. Nebuchadnezzar, commander of the imperial guard, carried into exile to Babylon the people who remained in the city, along with those who had gone over to him, and the rest of the people. (Jeremiah 39:1,8-9, NIV)

Nebuchadnezzar, the king of Babylon, went to Jerusalem and besieged it:

> Then the king ordered Ashpenaz, chief of his court officials, to bring into the king's service some of the Israelites from the royal family and the nobility—young men without any physical defect, handsome, showing aptitude for every kind of learning, well informed, quick to understand, and qualified to serve in the king's palace. (Daniel 1:3-4, NIV)

From these young men the king would choose the best to serve him in the royal palace and his kingdom. We have a detailed description of who Daniel was. He was from nobility and very handsome, highly intelligent, and quick to learn and understand. During the siege of Jerusalem, Daniel was 17 years old. He was brought to Babylon in chains as a slave. Before this event, he had everything going for him in his life in Jerusalem. His family would have planned for a prosperous and bright future for him among the royalty of the Jews. They would have planned for a prominent position in leadership in the future, marriage, and family. His days would have been filled with family and friends, and he would have participated in all the holy days and religious events that all the Israelites celebrated in the magnificent temple of the Lord.

We know that he was a devout Jew and loved the Lord because after he was chosen to be a slave in the king's palace, he resolved not to defile himself with the royal food and wine that had been offered him (see Daniel 1:8). This stand for his faith could have cost him his life. Daniel and three other young men were chosen out of all the others to enter the king's service. "The king talked with them, and he found none equal to Daniel, Hananiah, Mishael and Azariah; so they entered the king's service" (Daniel 1:19, NIV).

They were living in the country of their cruel, ungodly enemies in an evil, pagan land. They had lost every possession, and during the siege of Jerusalem they would have witnessed firsthand the murder of friends and family, the burning of their homes, and the destruction of their beloved magnificent temple of God. They lost all rights to their freedom and were made eunuchs to serve in the king's palace.

They now had to serve as slaves to the wicked, pagan king, Nebuchadazzar, who was personally responsible for everything that had just happened to them. He had taken away everything from them and everyone whom they loved.

These bright, handsome, promising young men with their future ahead of them lost everything. How could this be God's plan for their lives?

One day King Nebuchadazzar had a dream, and he called on his astrologers, magicians, enchanters, and sorcerers to tell him what he dreamed and what it meant. God had given Daniel the gift of dream interpretation. The Lord knew that this was a tool that Daniel would need and that it would bring glory to God. When the Lord calls us, He also equips us for the assignment. None of the wise men could tell the king what he dreamed and the meaning of the dream. This enraged the king.

He issued a decree that if none of these wise men could interpret the dream, they would all be put to death. It did not take long for the Lord to orchestrate these circumstances to direct the king's attention to Daniel and reveal himself to this king. Daniel and his three friends—Hananiah, Mishael, and Azariah—prayed to the Lord and pleaded for mercy so that they might not be executed with the rest of the wise men of Babylon.

At this time, I do not think that Daniel had any idea that the results would be as spectacular and far reaching as the Lord had planned. During the night, the mystery and meaning of the dream was revealed to Daniel in a vision (see Daniel 2:19). Daniel praised the God of heaven because He answered his prayer, and their lives would be spared. The next morning Daniel told the king the meaning of his dream.

> Praise be to the name of God for ever and ever; wisdom and power are His. He changes times and seasons; He sets up kings and deposes them. He gives wisdom to the wise and knowledge to the discerning. He reveals deep and hidden things; He knows what lies in darkness and light dwells with Him. I thank and praise you O God, of my fathers; You have given me wisdom and power, you have made known to me what we asked of You . . . You have made known to us the dream of the king. (Daniel 2:19-23, NIV)

> The king asked Daniel (also called Belteshazzar), "Are you able to tell me what I saw in my dream and interpret it?" Daniel replied, "No wise man, enchanter, magician or diviner can explain to the king the mystery he has asked about, but there is a God in heaven who reveals mysteries. He has shown King Nebuchadnezzar what will happen in days to come." (Daniel 2:26-28, NIV)

Daniel told the king that this mystery was revealed not because of Daniel's great wisdom but because God wanted to show him his future.

> God has shown the king what will take place in the future. . . ." Then King Nebuchadnezzar fell prostrate before Daniel and paid him honor and ordered that an

offering and incense be presented to him. The king said to Daniel, "Surely your God is the God of gods and the Lord of kings and a revealer of mysteries, for you were able to reveal this mystery." (Daniel 2:45-47, NIV)

It brought great glory to God. Daniel was spared from execution with the other wise men. "Then the king placed Daniel in a high position and lavished many gifts on him. He made him ruler over the entire province of Babylon and placed him in charge of all its wise men" (Daniel 2:48, NIV).

However, the fact remained that he was exiled in a land far from home and living as a slave under the rule of his enemies. Daniel was a servant and slave to four different kings in his lifetime. He endured all kinds of hardships, cruelty, humiliation, and persecution for his faith in the God of Israel.

I used to think that Daniel was a young man when he was facing the lions' den—maybe because of Sunday school stories I heard as a child. The enemy never stopped trying to rob, steal, and destroy him. The fact is that after more than 60 years of service to these kings, we see that there were still wicked men who were scheming to destroy Daniel because they were jealous of him. He was a totally godly man and was faithfully serving the king. Daniel was over 80 years old when his enemies devised this plan to take his life.

The king at the time was King Darius, and he had appointed 120 rulers (satraps) throughout his kingdom "with three administrators over them, one of whom was Daniel" (see Daniel

6:1-2).

"Now Daniel so distinguished himself among the administrators and the satraps by his exceptional qualities that the king planned to set him over the whole kingdom" (Daniel 6:3, NIV).

Daniel served under four ungodly kings in a foreign, pagan country all these years, but he still was distinguished over all the others as the best in the nation.

He was being watched by all the administrators who King Darius appointed to help run the kingdom. These men were jealous of Daniel, and they conspired to destroy his reputation and his life.

> At this, the administrators and satraps tried to find grounds for charges against Daniel in his conduct of government affairs, but they were unable to do so. They could find no corruption in him, because he was trustworthy and neither corrupt nor negligent. Finally these men said, "We will never find any basis for charges against this man Daniel unless it has something to do with the law of his God." (Daniel 6:4-5, NIV)

Then they all agreed to go to King Darius and request that he issue a royal decree that anyone who prayed to anyone else except King Darius for the next thirty days would be thrown into the lions' den. They had seen Daniel in his window praying on his knees three times a day to the Lord his God. It was the perfect trap, they thought. Daniel was a totally innocent man, and he had done nothing to cause this attack. These men were totally evil in their plan to destroy him.

Daniel could have fled for his life and hidden. This sounds like a good idea when it looks like there is no way out. He could have just prayed in secret for 30 days. It would not be like he stopped praying, right?

Daniel chose to believe in God and allow all the people to witness his trust in the loving, mighty, powerful God he served. He was more concerned about God's reputation than his own or even his own life. This trial was not about what a righteous man Daniel was; it was about what a loving and faithful God he served.

"Be still before the Lord and wait patiently for him; do not fret when people succeed in their ways, when they carry out their wicked schemes" (Psalm 37:7, NIV). This verse clearly states that there will be times when evil men succeed in their schemes.

God was right there with Daniel when he was thrown in the lions' den. Everyone in the kingdom had heard of what happened to Daniel and that his God did not show up to save him from punishment, to stop these men or prevent the evil plot from being carried out. Daniel had been hurled into the lions' den. Everyone would have thought, *It is too late now. It looks like the God of Daniel failed to protect and rescue him from this fatal attack.*

However, the next morning came, and King Darius ran to

the lions' den, calling out to Daniel. He was holding on to the hope that what Daniel had told him about his God was true. The next verses are some of my personal favorites in Scripture. In the most hopeless of situations, "Daniel answered, 'May the king live forever! My God sent his angel, and he shut the mouths of the lions. They have not hurt me, because I was found innocent in his sight. Nor have I ever done any wrong before you, Your Majesty'" (Daniel 6:21-22, NIV).

"And when Daniel was lifted from the den, no wound was found on him, because he had trusted in his God" (v. 23, NIV). Not even a scratch from the fall! Daniel was over 80 years old, and he had survived the fall into the lions' den with no broken bones, not even a scratch, and God miraculously delivered him from hungry lions.

Daniel could have been tempted to question the Lord's love for him and doubt God's ability to save him. He had served the Lord with all his heart these 80 years and suffered so much. He could have said to the Lord, "It is too much! Why do I have to go through this? I am old, and I am tired of being attacked." But Daniel saw it as the opportunity of a lifetime to show the whole nation and all his enemies that his God was the true God, and He was able to rescue, save, and avenge him.

I find that these next verses are some of the most powerful and faith-filled words of Scripture. They were spoken to the whole world:

> Then King Darius wrote to all the nations and people of every language in all the earth: "May you prosper greatly! I issue a decree that in every part of my kingdom people must fear and reverence the God of Daniel. For he is the living God and he endures forever; his kingdom will not be destroyed, his dominion will never end. He rescues and he saves; he performs signs and wonders in the heavens and on the earth. He has rescued Daniel from the power of the lions." (Daniel 6:25-27, NIV)

God showed up at the perfect time for Daniel to have the maximum impact on King Darius and on every person in the whole kingdom. In God's kingdom, there is always a bigger picture and a bigger plan, and everything that happens in our lives is an opportunity for the people around us to see what an awesome God we serve.

Do you find yourself in a lifelong battle with someone or something that has labeled you for defeat and exile?

Has the enemy told you that you will never be free and never have victory over "this"? We need to view our circumstances from above, where the Lord dwells and His sovereign control is over all. We live in a sinful and fallen world, and we have an enemy that wants to enslave and carry us off into exile. The Lord has a plan for us, and His purpose is to show the light of His salvation to a lost and dying world. This is the exact place where the Lord wants to shine His light in this dark and hopeless place, where there is no love. God is looking for someone who will go and shine there.

If Daniel had been able to stay in Jerusalem, and Nebuchadnezzar had not destroyed Jerusalem, Daniel would have been able to continue with his life as a Jewish leader and prosperous man among his people. But what would have happened to the pagan nation of Babylon and all the wicked and lost peoples of these lands? The Lord knew that it would take the sacrifice and suffering of His children to reach these people; there was no other way.

We have all experienced to one degree or another sacrifice and unfair and unjust suffering because of the sins of others. We live out our life and testimony before the eyes of our enemies and the world.

Through the suffering and death of Jesus, we are given a full pardon if we believe in Him and put our faith in Him. We are rescued and delivered from eternal death. Just like King Darius and the people of that time, God wants to show His faithfulness and love to a lost and dying world.

Jesus is alive because the Spirit of God has resurrected Him and given Him a place at the right hand of God the Father in heaven. He has won the victory over all our enemies and has been given all power and authority (see 1 Peter 3:22). Today, we have been given the command to share this good news. Now we have the privilege to show the world what a faithful, loving, and powerful God we serve.

Daniel's God is our God too, and He still works signs and wonders. He still rescues and saves those who put their trust in

Him. Even in the most hopeless and impossible circumstances, even when it looks like it is too late, the Lord can rescue, deliver, and bring victory.

Sometimes I struggle to see my trials and suffering as the "opportunity of a lifetime" to show the world what the Lord can do. When I have been in situations that are ongoing, quite frankly I have struggled to keep my eyes on the bigger picture and all the lives that the Lord wanted to touch through my testimony. Daniel gives me renewed courage and helps me get my eyes back on Jesus. I have not yet given up and lost as much as he lost, and no trial or struggle has gone on as long as Daniel's. This humble man persevered and stayed strong all his life, and even at 80 years old, he still saw his trials as the opportunity of a lifetime. This is the greatest testimony to the keeping power of God. There is hope and encouragement for all of us that we serve the same mighty God and loving Father. He will work in our lives as He did in Daniel's.

Do not believe the lies of the enemy that the Lord is not able to keep you strong and faithful. "To him who is able to keep you from stumbling and to present you before his glorious presence without fault and with great joy—to the only God our Savior be glory, majesty, power and authority, through Jesus Christ our Lord, before all ages, now and forevermore! Amen" (Jude 1:24, NIV).

It is Jesus who will keep us from falling, presenting us to the Father in heaven blameless and holy because of His power, and it will give Him great joy. Make no mistake, it is His sovereign will. He will receive the glory for it all—past, present, and future victory.

I believe that the most amazing miracle that the Lord works in our lives is giving us the grace, strength, and endurance to stay strong under all circumstances. Daniel's rescue from the lions' den was spectacular and dramatic, but I believe that the greater testimony and miracle was the power of God keeping him all those years, giving him strength and perseverance. His life was a light for all to see, and his impact on those around him was profound. We will never know how many people turned to his God because of his life and his strong testimony over all those years. He let his light shine before the people so they could see his good works, and God was glorified in him (see Matthew 5:16). His testimony was not about all the blessings God poured out on him but how faithful and good God was to him all his life.

Maybe the Lord is using your life as a strong testimony to His love and faithfulness as He carries you and keeps you strong through a lifetime of struggles and trials. Maybe the Lord will use you to demonstrate a dramatic rescue and deliverance in front of all the world.

Paul boasts about his struggles and the word the Lord gave him: "'My grace is sufficient for you, for my power is made perfect in weakness.' Therefore I will boast all the more gladly about my weaknesses, so that Christ's power may rest on me. That is why, for Christ's sake, I delight in weakness, in insult, in hardships, in persecutions, in difficulties. For when I am weak, then I am strong" (2 Corinthians 12:9-10, NIV).

I encourage you to keep your eyes on Jesus. Do not look away for a minute.

The Lord will work everything in your life for your good, even the things that seem evil and wrong (see Romans 8:28). It cannot hinder or prevent God's purposes. He weaves the dark thread along with the light into the tapestry of our lives. The finished results will bring Him glory, honor, and praise. As you meditate on the life of this man Daniel, be assured that the plans that the Lord has for your life are just as important and far reaching. Most of us will never see what the Lord has worked through our lives, but we will see it all when we get to heaven.

My dear sisters and brothers, be strong and of good courage. Keep asking in prayer and always stay in the Word. Build yourself up in faith, and do not give up. Your reward is great! Some day you will fall at His feet in humble gratitude as you view your whole life story in living color. You will see clearly, and then it will all make perfect sense. You will hear His loving voice say, "Well done, good and faithful servant!" (Matthew 25:21, NIV).

You will enter into your reward that will so surpass anything that your heart or mind could ever believe or dream of.

Chapter 13

DON'T WORRY ABOUT YOUR LIFE

Jesus spent most of His time during His early ministry teaching and demonstrating His Father's faithfulness. The people who spent time with Jesus had all their needs met. He fed them when they were hungry; He healed the sick. They experienced God's love and power coming from Him.

The Father wants us to live free from anxiety and worry, experiencing peace and rest in His loving arms. Jesus said, "Therefore I tell you, do not worry about your life, what you will eat, or drink; or about your body, what you will wear. Isn't life more than food, and the body more than clothes?" (Matthew 6:25, NIV).

Our most basic needs as humans are food and water. We need nourishment and water every day. Jesus said that if we drink His living water, we will never thirst again (see John 4:14). The Lord is the one who satisfies all our thirst, body, soul, and spirit. He nourishes and sustains us. He provides life-giving water to all He has made. The Lord has provided oceans, rivers, and mountain streams to water the earth, as well as rain.

When Jesus spoke of the life-giving spiritual water that He gives, it will satisfy all our emotional and spiritual needs. He promised to heal the brokenhearted and bind up all our wounds, carry all our burdens, and satisfy our longing hearts with good things (see Psalm 147:3). He also promised to strengthen those who are weak and comfort those who mourn (see Matthew 5:4).

The scriptures below are weapons that can help you silence the whispers that you hear in your mind telling you to worry and be afraid. These are verses you can speak out loud and declare over yourself as God's truth:

My whole being will exclaim, "Who is like you, Lord? You rescue the poor from those too strong for them." (Psalm 35:10, NIV)

The Lord is close to the brokenhearted and saves those who are crushed in spirit. (Psalm 34:18, NIV)

The Lord . . . delights in the well-being of his servant. (Psalm 35:27, NIV)

Great peace have those who love your law, and nothing can make them stumble. (Psalm 119:165, NIV)

Though I walk in the midst of trouble, you preserve my life. (Psalm 138:7, NIV)

Are not five sparrows sold for two pennies? Yet not one of them is forgotten by God. (Luke 12:6, NIV)

This is such a powerful statement about the love and faithfulness of God. God does not forget about even one sparrow He has created; not one falls to the ground without Him seeing it happen. I have trouble even getting my mind around this knowledge and truth. Then after this statement, Jesus says, "Indeed, the very hairs of your head are all numbered. Don't be afraid; you are worth more than many sparrows" (Luke 12:7, NIV).

The Lord is in complete control and on top of every event and everything He has created, especially in the lives of His own children. Why do we worry about this life and the things of this earth so much?

We spend so much of our time and energy trying to protect and care for the things of this life. The Lord, in His infinite love, desires to free us from the worry and anxiety that this causes us. He wants us to enter into His rest. How much more clearly can He tell us that He is more than able to take care of all our needs?

The scriptures say the hair on our heads are numbered; this seems like such an unnecessary task for the Lord to bother doing. When we look around at all the problems and evil in this world, why would the Lord ever waste precious time counting the hairs on our head every day?

I believe that the Father has such a passionate heart and desire to express His deep love for us that He demonstrates this love with an act that is so beyond anything that anyone else would ever think to do. It is a vivid and tender view of the immeasurable, unsearchable love the Father has for His children.

In Luke 12:24 Jesus says, "Consider the ravens: They do not sow or reap, they have no storeroom or barn; yet God feeds them. And how much more valuable you are than birds" (NIV).

Jesus makes a statement in the very next verses that should really challenge us when we are stressing, working to survive, and struggling to provide for our needs in this material world: "Who of you by worrying can add a single hour to his life? Since you cannot do this very little thing, why do you worry about the rest?" (vv. 25-26, NIV).

Jesus knows that we can be anxious and worried, losing sleep over how we are going to make it. Whether practically (concerning lack and loss of worldly things), emotionally, or spiritually, we find ourselves crying out to God and struggling with our thoughts and feelings. We question whether or not He will provide the comfort and protection we need. Jesus took time to talk about and explain the Father's love with these scriptures so that our fearful, restless hearts would find comfort and quiet.

The Lord wants to free us from all the snares and traps the enemy has laid to trip us up. The devil tries to get us to focus on all the visual signs and events to get our eyes off Jesus. He always accuses God of not caring about us or taking care of us. God wants to reassure us that He is in complete control. I have heard it from multiple sources that the words "fear not" are written in the Bible 365 times—one for each day of the year. This is no coincidence; the Lord knew that our struggle with fear would be a daily battle.

There have been times when I have taken my eyes off the Lord because of discouragement and frustration from praying and waiting so long for the answer. I have struggles with an anxious heart over the salvation of a loved one. I have found it hard to stand in faith, wait, and just rest in the Lord, especially when I know that what I am asking is in His will. I have been praying for over forty years for some people in my life. It seems so urgent to me for them to experience Jesus, all His love and saving power, to change their lives. I was patient and full of faith for about the first year or two. But as the years went by, my faith started to falter, and I could not believe that the Lord would wait so long.

I knew that it is God's passionate desire that all men come to Him and be saved. So why was nothing happening? I prayed so fervently and faithfully for so many years but still did not see change.

What do I do with my restless, anxious heart when the answer does not come and the prayer seems to go unanswered? The Lord has given me all these scriptures and insight that I am sharing with you to calm and quiet my heart. I have learned to use these verses many times over the years to get my eyes back on Him. All these scriptures reassure my soul and reveal the true heart of God. They dispel all the lies and accusations about Him, coming like arrows into my mind. The same loving, caring Father whom these verses describe is the one who is watching over my life and holds the answer to my prayers for these people in His hands. I will both hope and quietly wait for the salvation of the Lord.

Jesus continues to teach and explain, "And why do you worry about clothes? See how the flowers of the field grow. They do not labor or spin. Yet I tell you that not even Solomon in all his splendor was dressed like one of these" (Matthew 6:28-29, NIV).

Jesus was talking about how the flowers grow. Before we even see them pop out of the ground or smell their rich fragrance or see their bright, beautiful blossoms and petals, the Lord is taking care of them from the time they are only seeds in the ground. The Lord is also nurturing and doing all the work in our lives from the day that we are planted in His garden. He is faithfully providing everything necessary for the lilies to become mature flowers in all their splendor. What a beautiful picture of what He is doing in us as well. He is the Creator, planter, and husbandman who does all the work to bring us into maturity and full bloom.

I do not know what Solomon, the king of Israel, looked like or what his royal garments, jewels, and crowns were like, but I can only imagine that he must have been lavishly and richly dressed beyond anything that existed in those days, or maybe ever since. His wealth and resources were limitless. He would have hired the most creative, artistic, and talented designers and tailors to make all his royal garments. Jesus was saying that even if you could hire and bring together all the most famous and talented artists and designers of the world and give them unlimited resources and money to make garments, jewelry, crowns, and clothing for us—the children of the King—it would pale in comparison to the beauty and splendor of what the Lord wants to do with our lives.

I do not think we can fully comprehend how lavishly and richly the Lord wants to clothe us. We are being fashioned and prepared for eternity with Him. The garments He has fashioned will cover all the scars, flaws, and imperfections. His glorious robes and rich fabrics are designed to display His beauty in us. Ezekiel 16:8-14 describes how the bride of the King of kings will be dressed and adorned by Him. Please take the time to read these verses by yourself and let God speak to you through them.

As we meditate on and really ponder these verses and imagine what our robes and garments look like in the spirit realm, we can begin to see that we are indeed covered and beautiful in the eyes of God. If God cares enough to take a dead seed lying in the dirt, give it life, and cause it to grow into a breathtakingly beautiful flower only to bloom for a few days, how much more will He make His own children, who will live forever, to be breathtakingly beautiful? This is His heart's desire. We were created for Him.

Do not let the enemy lead you down that path of worry and anxiousness. If we allow ourselves to focus on our flaws, it can also lead us to try to cover them up. We worry about what others think of us and how they perceive us. This path creates more anxiety because we begin to fear that the truth will come out, that people will discover our weaknesses and shortcomings. We start believing in our hearts that we have to work to measure up in our own strength and power. It is a slippery slope, and the devil is able to provide all the proof we need by manipulating people and circumstances around us to support the lies he is telling us. He has more than enough people at his disposal to work for him in his evil schemes.

Jesus commands us, "So do not worry, saying, 'What shall we eat?' Or 'What shall we drink?' or 'What shall we wear?' For the pagans run after all these things, and your heavenly Father knows that you need them. But seek first his kingdom and his righteousness, all these things will be given to you as well" (Matthew 6:31-33, NIV).

We are heirs of His whole kingdom. God is not telling us that all material blessings are bad, that we are to be poor and homeless. These things in themselves are not bad, and they are all blessings and provision from our heavenly Father. Every good and perfect gift is from above and comes from God (see James 1:17). Do not set your heart on things that give only temporary satisfaction. If we focus on these things and put them first, it will leave us hungry and thirsty for the true eternal things from God.

He is the one who truly satisfies our every need. The focus is to be on Jesus, His kingdom, and our relationship with Him. To abandon our whole life to His sovereign plans and purposes and to make Him King and Lord of our hearts is to let Him be number one and reign in our lives. Afterward, we can add the earthly, temporal things of this world and enjoy them as blessings from our Father who loves us. Whether we have a lot or truly little, we will always be rich in the Lord. Life is so short, and yet it is such an amazing, glorious testimony to the Creator's love and care.

We are called His "little flock." We are compared to sheep that are totally helpless and unable to take care of themselves or provide for any of their needs. The Lord is letting us know that He is willing and able to provide for us just like a shepherd does for his helpless sheep. What a tenderhearted expression from our loving Father. "Do not be afraid, little flock, for your Father has been pleased to give you the kingdom" (Luke 12:32, NIV).

God is telling us that we are to look at the animals—the birds and the flowers and all creation—and we will see how powerful He is and recognize all His eternal qualities of love, care, and faithfulness. This whole world will one day pass away. It was all created for a season and time that is temporary. If the Lord has taken so much love and care to create so much for just a season, we will never be able to imagine what amazing things He has planned for us that are eternal and to share with Him forever in His heavenly kingdom. What will the new heaven and Earth be like? We do not know now, but I am sure it will far surpass anything we have ever seen or known.

"For since the creation of the world God's invisible qualities—his eternal power and divine nature—have been clearly seen, being understood from what has been made so that people are without excuse" (Romans 1:20, NIV).

The Lord talks about the garments that His children are to be adorned and dressed in. Just like the flowers and the endless beauty of His creation, He desires that we display His glory and endless love for us before the world!

"Be dressed ready for service and keep your lamps burning, like servants waiting for their master to return from a wedding banquet, so that when he comes and knocks they can immediately open the door for him" (Luke 12:35, NIV).

"Therefore, as God's chosen people, holy and dearly loved, clothe yourselves with compassion, kindness, humility, gentleness and patience. Bear with each other and forgive one another if any of you has a grievance you may have against someone. Forgive as the Lord forgave you. And over all these virtues put on love, which binds them together in perfect unity" (Colossians 3:12-14, NIV).

When we look at the beauty of breathtaking gardens, bursting with color and every shape and size of flowers, our response is not "I wish I could be a beautiful flower!" Instead, we are in awe and wonder at the Creator of such detail and amazing beauty. If we see magnificent tropical birds with vibrant rich feathers of every color in the rainbow, we do not envy them and go out and buy feathers to dress like them. God has a unique and specific design and purpose for everything and everyone. All of God's creation glorifies Him and is meant to show how carefully and wonderfully created everything on Earth is. From the smallest insect or even plankton to the redwood tree or the great white whale, each has been created with purpose.

This is God's plan and purpose for our lives. His plans *never* fail! He will accomplish this very thing in our lives, no matter how impossible that sounds. He said it and I believe it. Amen.

When I read about the Lord counting the hairs on my head, I can picture Him next to me. If I think about how close someone would have to get in order to count each hair, I imagine Him so close that I could feel His breath against my cheek. As I am sitting there with Him, He begins to count. I know that He has the time because He has already been taking care of all the important things in my life.

The Bible doesn't say He does this every day; however, since the number of hairs changes every day, it would be a daily task. If He never fails to do this small, seemingly meaningless task, how could He possibly fail to take care of all the other things in my life? Could you even imagine anyone on Earth wanting to count the hairs on your head every day? I am sure that it has never been done by anyone or ever will be. A love like this the world has never known!

If you are discouraged today and feeling lonely or unloved, kneel down and spend time waiting on the Lord. With your spiritual eyes, picture the Lord counting each hair, and let Him minister comfort and reassurance of His love as you rest in His loving arms for a while. Let Him come and fill you with His peace.

The Father sent Jesus to come and live a perfect life because He knew that we could not. Jesus dealt with all evil and sin, making payment in full. He has opened up to us the way of peace and a new life. This newness is a glorious life that is free from guilt, shame, and failure because we are robed in His righteousness and covered in His blood. We are to honor and glorify the Lord with our faith and trust in Him. We do not need to be disappointed because we are sometimes weak and become fearful; this is part of our fallen nature. It is what we do with our weakness and fears that makes the difference. All through the Bible, God tells us to take courage and to not be afraid. He reassures us that He is greater than all our fears. In Christ Jesus, we can triumph over our fears through His resurrection power and Spirit.

"Come to Me all you who are weary and burdened, and I will give you rest" (Matthew 11:28, NIV).

We have a Savior who is waiting for us to bring all our fears and anxiety to Him, to the foot of the cross, and lay it down there. Maybe it would be helpful to write down on a piece of paper what you are struggling with and literally lay it down where you spend your time with the Lord in prayer. I have a prayer closet, and there are many notes and papers with the cares of my life written down. Each day of the year, I have to let the Lord impart to me the courage to leave them with Him. There is always the temptation to start to worry and go back down that path again, but I find it easier to talk myself into leaving them all with the Lord when I see them literally written down on paper where I meet with Him every day. "For God hath not given us a spirit of fear but of power and of love and of a sound mind" (2 Timothy 1:7, KJV).

Worry and anxiety always attract a spirit of fear from our enemy, the devil. John tells us that perfect love casts out all fear (see 1 John 4:18). Jesus is that perfect love! He has the power to cast out fear, and we have been given the authority through Christ to cast it out. However, if we entertain it, it will not leave. If we ignore it, it will not leave. If we try to fight it with our own strength and resolve, it will not leave. The power to overcome and make it flee is through faith in Jesus' name and the power of His blood.

My prayer for you is that in all the trials and circumstances that are going on in your life today, the Lord will fill you with His spirit of love, power, and sound mind. I pray that you will be given supernatural courage to overcome worry and fear and the faith to believe that He is able to take care of your every need. I pray God will use the verses in this book to speak life and hope into your battle-weary heart. They are living words, and they are alive in my spirit because He has brought me victory many times through these very verses. In all your weakness, let Him show you in a miraculous way just how much He loves you and how mighty and powerful He really is. Let it be a mighty testimony of victory that you can share with others and encourage them. To God be the glory!

Chapter 14

BREAD AND WATER IN THE WILDERNESS

Our walk and journey through life today are much the same as the desert wilderness that the Israelites walked through long ago. When we receive Jesus, we are delivered and set free from the slavery and bondage of the prince of this world, Satan. We then enter into a spiritual wilderness and begin the long process of discovering who God is and learning to trust and depend on Him. What the Lord wants to teach us is to walk in a supernatural way and to stop depending on our own strength, power, or the things of this world to provide for any of our needs.

In the book of Exodus we read the account of the Israelites, their bondage in Egypt, the Lord's plan of deliverance through His servant Moses, and their journey through the wilderness. When the Israelites left Egypt and entered the desert, they thought they had plenty of food, that it would be plenty to last for the three-day journey to Canaan, the promised land flowing with milk and honey. The Lord knew these newly freed slaves were not ready to take possession of this land that He had promised. They needed much training and teaching to transform them into sons and daughters of the King. These slaves were to become His heirs and must fight as skilled warriors, learning to destroy all their enemies, before they could rule and reign in this new kingdom. It would require much time to accomplish all this in their lives.

More important was the process of learning and receiving from the Lord a whole new identity in Him and experiencing Him as a loving Father. These were things that they would have to learn from scratch and supernaturally. They did not know if God would be a cruel and angry ruler like Pharaoh and his gods. They had seen all the terrifying plagues and judgments God had inflicted against all the gods of Egypt. This is all they had experienced so far; it was all they had to go by.

The Lord made a lot of promises to them, but they didn't know if He would keep them. I would have been afraid and confused too if I was one of them. God did not take them directly to the promised land and give them everything they wanted and everything He promised. Because of His amazing love, He would take the time to patiently and slowly teach them about Himself and how to take possession of this new land. He led them through the wilderness for forty years because He wanted them to get to know Him and His great faithfulness and love. He wanted to teach them that He could supply every need and without any natural resources or provisions.

The food supply that they brought out of Egypt with them was produced by hard work and human hands, using seeds they planted in the ground and producing crops from the sweat of their brows, their natural strength and ability. Everyone knows that you cannot survive without food and water, especially out in a sun-scorched desert, and there is no way that anything will grow out there either. It is impossible. This journey took them into foreign territory, places where they had never traveled, not just literally but also in the spiritual realm. The Israelites never experienced walking in faith and trusting the Lord when they were in Egypt. They were dependent upon Pharaoh and Egypt for everything. They totally relied on human resources for their needs, and their own strength, abilities, and talents.

The Lord was about to show them a new way of living and teach them how to depend on Him. This has deep spiritual application in our lives today and in the seasons and times we are in right now. When we enter into a personal and real relationship with God through His Son, Jesus, we all start out with many questions and wonder who this God is who has come and set us free. We do not know anything about Him yet. This is an extremely critical lesson we must learn if we are to grow and mature in the Lord.

"Then Moses led Israel from the Red Sea and they went into the Desert of Shur. For three days they traveled in the desert without finding water" (Exodus 15:22, NIV).

The first crisis happened to the Israelites only three days out in the desert. They ran out of water, and they were in the middle of the parched desert, nothing but sand for miles in every direction. The Israelites looked to a man, Moses, just like they had done all their lives back in Egypt, and said, "You need to provide water for us! We are going to die out here." To them it looked like God had brought them out there to die of thirst. They did not know God or trust Him yet. All the while, the Lord was standing right there, His presence "bigger than life" in a great big ol' cloud that was protecting them from the heat and keeping them alive in the desert.

He was about to give them their first lesson about who He was. As we read further in Exodus 15, they came to Marah, where there was water, but it was bitter, and they could not drink it. It is interesting that the water that they needed to drink to stay alive was bitter, but when the Lord told Moses to take a piece of wood and throw it into the water, the water became sweet. Similarly, Christ's death on a wooden cross makes a way for the dirty, contaminated water of our lives to be made clean and pure.

They then traveled a little farther into the desert, and their next stop was an oasis called Elim (see Exodus 15:27). It had twelve springs of water, a shadow of the twelve vessels of water in the New Testament: the disciples. The Israelites enjoyed the natural refreshment and shade from this place for a while. Then they left Elim and came to the Desert of Sin. "In the desert the whole community grumbled against Moses and Aaron. The Israelites said to them, 'If only we had died by the Lord's hand in Egypt'" (Exodus 16:2, NIV).

This sounds just like another Israelite named Esau in the book of Genesis. When he was so driven by the lust for natural food to satisfy his hunger, he was willing to give up all his inheritance to his brother Jacob for a meager bowl of stew. Esau had the same disregard for the Lord and the inheritance he was given by God.

> Once when Jacob was cooking some stew, Esau came in from the open country, famished. He said to Jacob, "Quick, let me have some of that red stew! I'm famished!" ... Jacob replied, "First sell me your birthright." "Look, I am about to die," Esau said. "What good is the birthright to me?" Then Jacob gave Esau some bread and lentil stew. He ate and drank, and then got up and left. So Esau despised his birthright. (Genesis 25:29-32,34, NIV)

The Israelites were willing to give up on the promises and plans that God had for them and inheritance in the promised land for the food that they were used to eating in Egypt. The Israelites said, "There we sat around pots of meat and ate all the food we wanted, but you Moses have brought us out into the desert to starve this entire assembly to death" (Exodus 16:2b).

These people were saying that they would rather die in slavery than learn to live as sons and daughters of the Lord and to take possession of the inherited promised land. There is a key point that they expressed about their time of slavery in Egypt. They said that they got to eat all they wanted in Egypt. They were believing the lie that they were somehow in control of their lives there. Now they were beginning to feel that they had lost all control of their circumstances and lives in the desert with the Lord.

I no longer look at them with a critical spirit and judge them for their attitudes and behavior. The Lord has revealed my attitudes and shown me just how much I used to be like them.

As a Christian, there were many times that I held on to the old familiar comforts and pleasures of the world. I thought that the Lord was being too strict and unreasonable to ask me to give up my worldly pleasures and the comfort they provided, as if He was trying to take away things that I enjoyed and make me unhappy. I was blind and deceived, and I did not know that they were cheap substitutes for all the rich blessings, comforts, and provisions that He planned and wanted to pour out on me.

These worldly things were the very things that were hindering me from experiencing His supernatural power and presence. God patiently led and drew me away from the world, and I began to experience His amazing presence and provision. The more I tasted of the Lord's bounty in the spirit realm, the more my eyes were opened, and I could see how inadequate the things of the world were and how they never really gave me any lasting or sustaining happiness, peace, or satisfaction. In the end, I was always disappointed and dissatisfied.

Now I see them as worthless like Paul: "What is more, I consider everything a loss compared to the surpassing greatness of knowing Christ Jesus my Lord, for whose sake I have lost all things. I consider them rubbish, that I may gain Christ and be found in Him, not having a righteousness of my own that comes from the law, but that which is through faith in Christ—the righteousness that comes from God, and is by faith" (Philippians 3:8-9, NIV).

I still enjoy good friendships, recreation, and achievements, but they do not take first place anymore. My relationship with the Lord always comes first, and I know and have experienced His amazing love for me every day. Jesus has become the source for everything I want or need.

"Then the Lord said to Moses, 'I will rain down bread from heaven for you. The people are to go out each day and gather enough for that day. In this way I will test them and see whether they will follow my instructions'" (Exodus 16:4, NIV).

God took over complete control in a supernatural way again. They would receive heavenly manna each day from His hand. They were no longer going to get everything they wanted; they were going to learn to follow God's instructions because He had a better plan and purpose and knew so much more about what they really needed.

Moses told the Israelites about the manna, the bread that the Lord would send to feed them. He instructed them to go out each day and gather as much as they needed. "This is what the Lord has commanded: 'Everyone is to gather as much as they need. Take an omer for each person you have in your tent.'" The Israelites did as they were told; some gathered much, some little. And when they measured it by the omer, the one who gathered much did not have too much, and the one who gathered little did not have too little. Everyone had gathered just as much as they needed" (Exodus 16:16-18, NIV).

Before this, the people talked about having all the food they wanted, and now they would be going out and gathering all the food they needed. In the Lord's economy, their needs were measured and supplied in exact amounts. The Lord was in control because He alone knew what they needed and how much for each day's supply. There was a process of learning to trust and obey as they went out each day trusting that the Lord would provide from His rich storehouses in heaven everything that they would need for that day of their lives. This still is true today; we are to walk by faith each day and trust the Lord to supply for each need. Some days we do not need a lot, so the measure of grace and provision is measured out to match the needs. We all know that at other days in our lives, we need a truckload of grace, strength, power, and provision.

The Israelites tried to keep leftover manna for the next day, but it was full of maggots and began to smell. The leftover manna turned rancid and rotted. The Lord, in His wisdom and knowledge of the weakness of man, knows that we need to spend time every day in His Word, feeding on it and gathering strength and spiritual supply to meet the needs of that day.

Each day the provision is different. Do not worry that the small "omer of manna" you got today will be the same amount tomorrow. The Lord is personally measuring out the exact amount that we need—everything to nourish us and strengthen our frame with the exact amount in any category to match the issues, struggles, and lack we are experiencing that day. How I have wanted to carry into tomorrow the wonderful supply and bread from heaven that the Lord has provided on some of the tough days. In those difficult days, God matched them with such an abundance that I did not want to close my eyes to sleep those nights. As hard as the day was, it was so full of His presence that I did not want it to end. I wanted to somehow hold on to the manna and take some of it into the next day, even if I did not need as much—just to enjoy it and have an emergency supply.

Our spiritual "leftovers" from the previous days have no more power or life in them. They are stale. Our relationship with the Lord is to be a daily affair. First thing in the morning, we need to go and receive our daily bread from His hand. It's not about what we think we want that day but about trusting Him to provide what we need that day. It's about filling our hearts with the rich bounty of His Spirit and fellowship until we are full and satisfied.

Paul said to be anxious for nothing (see Philippians 4:6). Do not worry about the days ahead that could require much more supply than what we received today. This is such a powerful spiritual principle to learn in this. The Lord is the genius behind genius!

For forty years, the Israelites had to go out every morning and spend time gathering manna for that day. They were trusting the Lord to provide supernaturally because there were no other resources in the desert, nothing else to depend on, no one else to turn to. They were a captive audience. The Lord was teaching them, as a loving Father would, how to walk in the wilderness in His will and in His presence. They had to go and spend time gathering bread, taking it in, and feeding themselves and their family with it. "Give us this day our daily bread" (see Matthew 6:11) was the ancient lesson that every believer is still learning to walk in today.

We walk in faith and believe that the Lord will supply each day just what we need. As we grow up in the Lord, we make the shift from always asking for what we want to slowly allowing Him to supply what we need as our faith and trust in the Lord grow.

The Israelites did not know the Lord when they started this journey; they had no personal experience or knowledge of what He was like while they lived in Egypt. Over the forty years, they saw the cloud of His presence every day when they woke up, faithfully protecting them from the deadly heat of the Desert of Sin. Every morning the manna was there for them to gather and eat, as much as they needed.

Every evening they saw the pillar of fire appear to keep the predators away while they slept, to give them light in the total darkness, and to provide warmth for the freezing-cold desert nights. They were slowly learning about this amazing God who had chosen them as His children and would always be their God and Father. They were learning to trust and obey. This is an awfully slow process for all of us!

Our heavenly Father will never compromise our relationship with Him to give us what we think we want. His plans are so much bigger and better concerning our lives. First and foremost to God is our spiritual maturity and growth in faith. The children of Israel grumbled and complained whenever they were faced with any trial or challenge. The Lord supernaturally provided water for them to drink as they journeyed farther and farther into the desert. The Lord told Moses to take the staff and strike a rock and water would come out of it for the people to drink. All the Israelites watched the Lord miraculously provide water from a rock. In their minds, they knew that you cannot get water from a rock; it is impossible. With all of these miracles, God was after their hearts. This story is a foreshadow of Christ Jesus, the Living Water. When He was struck by the soldier while He hung on the cross, water came out of His side. He is the Rock that was struck so that we would not die of spiritual thirst in our journey through our deserts.

Here is a prophetic promise about Jesus the Messiah as the living water for His people:

> . . . strengthen the feeble hands, steady the knees that give way; say to those with fearful hearts; Your God will come . . . Then will the lame leap like a deer, and the tongue of the dumb shout for joy. Water will gush forth in the wilderness and streams in the desert. The burning sand will become a pool. (Isaiah 35:3-4,6-7, NIV)

God's "wilderness" is not meant to be a hot and lifeless desert where we experience severe hunger and thirst and are led around in uncertainty and all alone. He is not an angry and holy God who does not understand or care about us. This is what the devil likes to whisper in our ears: "If you follow the Lord, he will make you give up everything." The truth is, the only things that we will lose are the worthless rubbish and hindrances that are standing in the way of the Lord lavishing on us spiritual blessings far beyond what we could ask for or imagine!

The Lord always leaves the choice to us. We can stay in Egypt if we desire, and He will not force us to leave. Or we can choose to follow Him into the wilderness that leads to the promised land. There is no doubt that it is a long and difficult trip, but you will never hear one person in heaven who has finished the journey say, "It was not worth all the struggle and sacrifice to arrive at this glorious destination, the promised land." Many of us who are still on the journey here on Earth can also testify to the truth and reality that we have experienced a real taste of the promised land spiritually, right in the middle of the wilderness or surrounded by our enemies.

God's plan and purpose for our lives is to walk in close intimate fellowship with Him, to experience peace and joy every day, and to be fully satisfied as we drink of the Living Water and eat manna that Jesus provides through His Word. He has given us His Spirit to dwell inside us so that we can experience His presence and hear Him speak to us every day. My prayer for you is that you may be given the wisdom and revelation knowledge of your loving Father. Having Him reveal Himself and show you exactly what He is doing at this time in your life will help show you the direction you need to take. I pray for Him to give you a greater measure of faith and the courage and perseverance to keep following Him, even if you are walking in the middle of what may look like a barren wilderness right now. My prayer for you is simply to have a new supernatural, personal encounter with the Lord.

My life is a true testimony to God's faithfulness, perseverance, and patience to lead and guide me, even through the times when I wandered away from Him and when I got angry and rebelled, and the many times when I disappointed Him. How He has always lavished His love on me, even when I was unlovable. All the times when I was discouraged and wanted to give up, or did give up, and He brought me new hope and courage to go on. He always gives me time to mature and grow, to know Him better and trust Him more each day. God has been faithful to me. "Those who hope in Me will not be disappointed" (Isaiah 49:23b, NIV).

I am fully persuaded that *Jesus* is able to finish what He started in your life. Below is a power-anointed prayer that is the Word of God, and Paul prayed it for you and me years ago. Let's agree with him right now, and let the Lord work it out in our lives to the full measure that He desires.

Now may the God of peace, who through the blood of the eternal covenant brought back from the dead our

> Lord Jesus, that great Shepherd of the sheep, equip you with everything good for doing his will, and may he work in us what is pleasing to him, through Jesus Christ, to whom be glory for ever and ever. Amen. (Hebrews 13:20-21, NIV)

Before we end our time together, I'd like to leave you with some scriptures to encourage you in the wilderness you may be walking through.

> For I am the LORD your God who takes hold of your right hand and says to you, Do not fear; I will help you. (Isaiah 41:13, NIV)

> The poor and needy search for water, but there is none; their tongues are parched with thirst. But I the LORD will answer them; I, the God of Israel, will not forsake them. I will make rivers flow on barren heights, and springs within the valleys. I will turn the desert into pools of water, and the parched ground into springs. (Isaiah 41:17-18, NIV)

> Even to your old age and gray hairs I am he, I am he who will sustain you. I have made you and I will carry you; I will sustain you and I will rescue you. (Isaiah 46:4, NIV)

My prayer is that the Lord will watch over His Word to see it fulfilled in your life.

Other Books by Author

Book Available Now on Amazon
and most online bookstores